The Simple Investor: Financial Independence Without the Complexity

"A No-Fail Guide to Growing Your Wealth with Safe, Smart Investments — Even If You're Just Starting"

This book is a straightforward, accessible guide to achieving financial freedom through proven, low-risk investment strategies. Whether you're a beginner or just looking to simplify your approach, "The Simple Investor" breaks down essential investment concepts, from budgeting basics and setting realistic goals to navigating the stock market, understanding mutual funds, and even exploring real estate and retirement accounts. Each chapter provides practical, actionable advice on how to grow and protect your wealth, balance risk, and stay on track through all stages of life.

Through easy-to-understand explanations, relatable stories, and step-by-step strategies, this book empowers readers to take control of their financial future, build a diversified investment portfolio, and make informed choices with confidence. Start your journey to financial independence today, and discover how to build a sustainable, rewarding life through smart and simple investing.

Chapters:

- Introduction
- Chapter 1: The Basics of Investing
- Chapter 2: The Essentials of Safe Investing
- Chapter 3: Stock Market Fundamentals
- Chapter 4: Mutual Funds and ETFs
- Chapter 5: Retirement Accounts
- Chapter 6: Real Estate Investing
- Chapter 7: Risk Management and Insurance
- Chapter 8: Financial Independence and Legacy
- Final Chapter: A word of Advice and Grati

Introduction

For many, investing feels like navigating a dense jungle of complex terms, unpredictable markets, and intimidating concepts. Yet, financial independence is a goal that nearly everyone shares—a desire to feel secure, provide for loved ones, and live without the stress of paycheck-to-paycheck survival. It doesn't require insider knowledge or years of specialized training, but rather a straightforward approach, patience, and the commitment to make steady, well-informed decisions over time. Welcome to *The Simple Investor*, a guide designed to demystify the world of investing, so you can start growing your wealth confidently, even starting from scratch.

The Goal of Financial Independence

Financial independence means different things to different people. For some, it might mean saving enough to retire comfortably, while for others, it's about building a safety net that allows flexibility in career choices, or even providing a lasting legacy for family. However, at its core, financial independence is about choice. When you're financially secure, you can decide how and where to spend your time, whether that means pursuing a passion, starting a business, traveling, or simply reducing stress by having a robust emergency fund.

Our goal with *The Simple Investor* is to provide you with clear, actionable steps toward financial independence, regardless of your current knowledge or financial situation. By the end of this book, you will not only understand fundamental investment concepts but also feel confident in crafting and executing an investment plan tailored to your goals and risk tolerance.

Debunking the Complexity Myth

One of the biggest myths around investing is that it's too complicated for everyday people. Financial terms, fluctuating stock charts, and reports on economic indicators can indeed feel overwhelming, and financial advisors may seem to speak in a language all their own. But behind the jargon, the principles of sound investing are simpler than they appear. Anyone can learn to invest wisely by following a few basic principles.

Successful investing doesn't require an encyclopedic knowledge of markets or a deep dive into every trend. Many of the most effective strategies focus on consistency and patience rather than constant tweaking and analysis. You don't need to pick the next big stock or master complex financial theories. Instead, you need to understand how to set realistic goals, allocate your money across different types of assets to reduce risk and adopt a long-term mindset that keeps you focused on your personal financial goals.

What Does It Mean to Invest Simply?

To invest simply is to focus on the basics, avoid unnecessary risk, and remain consistent. The essence of simple investing is making sure that each financial decision serves a clear purpose. This approach includes choosing investment options that are known to yield steady returns, rather than pursuing high-risk assets that promise high rewards but could ultimately undermine your financial security.

For example, simple investing could mean choosing a low-cost index fund that mirrors the performance of the stock market over time. By doing so, you avoid the need to pick individual stocks, yet still benefit from overall market growth. Similarly, it could mean dedicating a portion of your money to bonds, real estate investment trusts (REITs), or other assets that offer relatively stable returns. These choices ensure that your investment plan remains manageable and grounded, allowing you to reach your goals without undue stress or complexity.

The most powerful aspect of simple investing is its accessibility. It doesn't matter if you're a high-earning professional or someone just starting with a modest income; the basic principles apply to everyone. Some of the best investors in history have proven that steady, conservative strategies often outperform more aggressive, high-stakes approaches. By focusing on these timeless principles, you can start investing with confidence, regardless of how much you currently know about the markets.

The Building Blocks of Financial Independence

Achieving financial independence is a journey that begins with small, consistent steps. Each chapter of this book will guide you through a critical component of your investment journey, helping you build a foundation that's strong and sustainable. Here's a brief overview of what you can expect:

- **Chapter 1: The Basics of Investing** will help you understand core concepts like compounding, risk, and diversification. We'll also explore why investing is a powerful way to protect and grow your wealth over time.
- **Chapter 2: The Essentials of Safe Investing** covers low-risk options and strategies for conservative growth. If you've ever worried about losing money in the markets, this chapter will help you feel comfortable with investments that are reliable and relatively stable.
- **Chapter 3: Stock Market Fundamentals** demystifies the stock market and introduces straightforward ways to benefit from long-term stock market growth without needing to become an expert.
- **Chapter 4: Mutual Funds and ETFs** introduces diversified investment vehicles that are ideal for beginning investors, allowing you to own a mix of assets with minimal research and management.

- **Chapter 5: Retirement Accounts** explains the benefits of tax-advantaged accounts, such as IRAs and 401(k)s, which can greatly accelerate your journey toward financial independence.
- **Chapter 6: Real Estate Investing** explores real estate options, from buying property to investing in Real Estate Investment Trusts (REITs), which offer exposure to the real estate market without the need to manage property directly.
- **Chapter 7: Risk Management and Insurance** focuses on protecting your wealth. We'll discuss how to handle risk appropriately and ensure that your investments remain secure, even in unpredictable times.
- **Chapter 8: Financial Independence and Legacy** provides guidance on crafting a plan for lifelong financial security and building a legacy for future generations.

Setting Your Intentions and Staying Committed

Before diving in, take a moment to reflect on your intentions for reading this book. What are your personal financial goals? Are you looking for freedom from debt, or do you envision a comfortable retirement? Maybe you want to establish financial security for your family or simply build an emergency fund that gives you peace of mind. By setting your intentions, you will have a clearer sense of purpose and a deeper commitment to the steps you'll learn throughout this book.

Consistency and patience are essential in the world of investing. Small, regular investments made over time are typically far more effective than large, sporadic ones. This book isn't about transforming your financial situation overnight; it's about helping you create a lasting, manageable plan that grows your wealth steadily and sustainably.

The Journey Begins

The journey to financial independence can seem daunting, but every step forward brings you closer to the life you envision. Whether you're looking to retire early, travel the world, or provide a stable foundation for your family, investing can be a powerful tool in turning those dreams into reality. This book will be your guide, walking you through each step with practical advice, clear explanations, and encouragement to stay the course.

So take a deep breath, set aside any fears or doubts, and prepare to embark on a journey toward financial freedom. Financial independence isn't reserved for the experts—it's within reach for everyone willing to invest in themselves. *The Simple Investor* will show you how. Let's get started.

Chapter 1: Foundations of Investing

Why Invest?

Investing is one of the most powerful tools for growing wealth, and it provides a pathway to achieving long-term financial goals. Unlike simply saving money, which generally preserves your cash for the short term, investing allows you to outpace inflation and grow your assets over time. This section will break down the key reasons for investing, focusing on the power of compounding, the importance of beating inflation, and the need to set well-defined goals to stay on track.

Building Wealth: The Power of Compounding, Beating Inflation, and Achieving Financial Goals

The Power of Compounding

The concept of compounding is one of the most essential principles in investing. Often referred to as "the eighth wonder of the world," compounding is the process by which your investment earnings generate additional earnings. Essentially, when you invest and earn a return, those returns are reinvested, allowing your investments to grow at an increasing rate over time.

Let's break down how it works with a simple example. Suppose you invest $1,000 at an annual return of 8%. After the first year, your investment grows by $80, giving you a total of $1,080. In the second year, you'll earn 8% on the new amount, which is $1,080. This means you'll earn $86.40, which is slightly more than the previous year's $80 return. Over time, as your investment continues to grow, compounding can result in exponential growth, which significantly increases the total value of your investment. The earlier you start investing, the more powerful compounding becomes, as the gains accumulate over a longer period.

Beating Inflation

Another critical reason to invest is to protect your wealth from inflation. Inflation refers to the gradual increase in the prices of goods and services over time, which reduces the purchasing power of money. For example, if inflation averages around 3% per year, the value of $100 today will be worth only about $97 next year in terms of purchasing power. This means that if you simply hold your money in cash or a low-interest savings account, the real value of your money will decrease over time.

Investing provides an opportunity to grow your money at a rate that outpaces inflation. While inflation typically ranges between 2% to 3% annually, the stock market has historically offered an average return of around 7% to 10% per year. By investing in assets that offer returns above the inflation rate, you can maintain and grow the real value of your wealth, ensuring that your financial resources don't diminish over time.

Achieving Financial Goals

Finally, one of the primary reasons to invest is to reach specific financial goals. Whether you're looking to buy a home, fund your child's education, or retire comfortably, investments allow you to accumulate the necessary capital to achieve these goals. Investing enables you to bridge the gap between your current financial position and where you want to be in the future. By setting clear financial targets and investing strategically, you can systematically work toward these objectives, making your financial dreams a reality.

Investing vs. Saving: Differences in Growth Potential, Risks of Inflation, and When to Save vs. Invest

Differences in Growth Potential

When it comes to building wealth, investing offers a significantly higher growth potential compared to traditional saving methods. Saving usually involves setting aside money in a low-risk, easily accessible account, such as a savings account or money market account, with a modest interest rate. These types of accounts are great for preserving capital and providing liquidity for short-term needs, but they don't offer the high returns typically associated with investing.

On the other hand, investing involves purchasing assets like stocks, bonds, or real estate with the expectation of generating a return. While investing carries some risk, it also has the potential for much higher returns than saving. For instance, a diversified stock portfolio could yield returns of 7% to 10% annually over the long term, whereas a savings account might only offer 0.5% to 2% per year. By investing, you can harness the growth potential of the markets to achieve substantial gains over time.

Risks of Inflation

As discussed earlier, inflation erodes the purchasing power of your money over time. Savings accounts and cash holdings, while safe from market risk, are vulnerable to inflation risk. If your savings only earn 1% interest and inflation is 3%, your real purchasing power is effectively shrinking each year. This means that by relying solely on savings, you may fall short of your long-term financial goals.

Investing, however, can help protect against inflation. By choosing assets that offer growth potential, such as stocks, real estate, or inflation-protected bonds, you can maintain and even increase your purchasing power over time. While investing involves some risk, the potential for inflation-beating returns makes it an essential component of a well-rounded financial plan.

When to Save vs. When to Invest

While investing offers greater growth potential, there are times when saving is more appropriate than investing. A good rule of thumb is to use savings for short-term goals or emergency funds and invest for long-term goals. For example, if you plan to make a large purchase within the next one to three years, keeping your money in a high-yield savings account provides security and easy access without the risk of market fluctuations.

However, if your goal is five, ten, or even twenty years away, investing is generally a better option. The longer your time horizon, the more you can tolerate the ups and downs of the market, and the more you can benefit from the power of compounding. By balancing saving and investing based on your timeline, you can optimize your strategy for both security and growth.

3. Setting Financial Goals: Creating Short-, Medium-, and Long-Term Goals; Using the SMART Goal Framework; and the Importance of Visualization

Creating Short-, Medium-, and Long-Term Goals

When it comes to investing, it's important to have clear, specific goals that can guide your decisions and keep you motivated. Short-term goals are typically objectives you plan to achieve within one to three years, such as building an emergency fund or saving for a vacation. Medium-term goals might span three to five years and could include buying a car or funding a down payment on a house. Long-term goals are those that require five years or more to achieve, such as saving for retirement or establishing a college fund for your children.

By categorizing your goals in this way, you can prioritize your investments and choose strategies that align with each timeline. Short-term goals may be best served by safer, more liquid assets like savings accounts or certificates of deposit (CDs), while long-term goals can benefit from more aggressive investments, such as stocks or mutual funds.

Using the SMART Goal Framework

The SMART goal framework—Specific, Measurable, Achievable, Relevant, and Time-bound—is a useful tool for setting clear financial objectives. Specificity helps you focus on a particular outcome (e.g., saving $10,000 for a down payment), while making your goal measurable allows you to track your progress. Setting achievable goals keeps you motivated and realistic about what you can accomplish based on your income and financial situation. Ensuring that your goal is relevant keeps it aligned with your overall financial plan, and setting a time-bound deadline gives you a concrete target date to work toward.

For example, rather than setting a vague goal like "I want to save money for a car," you might set a SMART goal: "I will save $5,000 over the next two years by putting $200 per month into a high-yield savings account." This specific, measurable, achievable, relevant, and time-bound goal helps you stay focused and disciplined.

The Importance of Visualization

Visualization is a powerful tool for maintaining motivation and staying on track with your financial goals. By creating a mental image of your goals, such as a future home, a comfortable retirement, or a debt-free life, you can reinforce your commitment and remain focused on the journey. Visualization can also help reduce the anxiety that sometimes comes with investing, as it reminds you of the purpose behind your financial decisions.

Consider creating a vision board or writing down your goals as a daily reminder of what you're working toward. By keeping your goals visible, you're more likely to stay disciplined and committed to achieving them, even during challenging times.

Investment Basics

When you begin to navigate the world of investing, understanding the basics is crucial to making informed decisions. In this section, we'll break down three fundamental concepts that every investor needs to grasp: assets and liabilities, risk and reward, and diversification. These are not just terms to memorize but practical ideas that can shape how you approach investing and help you build wealth with confidence.

Assets and Liabilities: Building Wealth the Right Way

Imagine you're an entrepreneur, starting with nothing but a dream and a small loan from your family. You open a bakery and, over time, you start making a profit. You reinvest that profit into expanding your business—buying better equipment, hiring staff, and opening new locations. All of these moves are investments that contribute to your wealth. In this scenario, your bakery represents an asset. It's something you own that generates value, whether it's the property, the equipment, or the customers who buy your products.

In the world of investing, assets are anything you own that has the potential to increase in value or generate income. Real estate, stocks, bonds, mutual funds, and even a successful business like your bakery are all examples of assets. The key to building wealth is to accumulate assets that grow over time, providing you with both income and appreciation in value.

Now, consider the flip side of your bakery: what if you accumulated too much debt in the early years? You might have borrowed money to purchase the building, bought expensive equipment on credit, or even taken out personal loans. While these might have helped you get started, they also represent liabilities—the money you owe to others. Liabilities, unlike assets, drain resources. Instead of generating income or increasing in value, they come with costs, like interest payments, that can slow down your path to financial independence.

The goal of any investor is to minimize liabilities and maximize assets. A simple way to think about this is: to focus on acquiring things that bring in money (assets) while managing or eliminating things that take money away (liabilities). For example, by paying off credit card debt or refinancing your mortgage, you're reducing your liabilities, freeing up more money to invest in assets that will grow your wealth over time.

A story that highlights the difference between assets and liabilities comes from a friend named Laura. Early in her career, she bought a car on credit because she thought it would help her get to work faster and look more professional. However, after a few months, she realized that the car wasn't just an expense—it was a liability. Between the car payments, insurance, and maintenance costs, she was pouring money into something that wasn't helping her grow wealth. Over time, Laura sold the car, paid off her debt, and started investing in stocks and index funds. As her assets grew, she was able to accumulate more wealth with less stress.

The key takeaway here is to carefully evaluate your assets and liabilities. By focusing on building assets that increase in value or produce income, you set yourself up for long-term financial success.

Risk and Reward: Finding Your Balance

Risk is a central part of investing. It's the price you pay for the potential of higher returns. However understanding how to manage risk is essential to growing your wealth while protecting your peace of mind. The key lies in balancing risk with reward, based on your risk tolerance.

Risk tolerance is the degree of risk you're willing to take on in your investments. It can vary greatly from person to person, and it often depends on factors like your age, financial goals, and personality. For example, a young professional in their 20s or 30s might be willing to take on more risk because they have time to recover from any losses. However, someone nearing retirement might want to take on less risk, as they don't have as much time to recoup losses before they need to start drawing from their investments.

Take the example of two investors: Sarah and Mark. Sarah is 25 years old and just starting her career. She is willing to take on higher-risk investments, such as stocks or cryptocurrencies, because she knows that she has time to ride out market fluctuations. She focuses on growth and isn't overly concerned about short-term volatility. On the other hand, Mark is 55 and wants to retire in 10 years. He's more conservative and prefers to invest in bonds or dividend-paying stocks, which offer steadier returns with less risk.

But here's the important part: Sarah and Mark's risk tolerance is not just about their age—it's also about their mindset. Sarah enjoys the thrill of investing in high-growth stocks and is comfortable with the idea that her portfolio might fluctuate wildly in the short term. Mark, on the other hand, finds the idea of watching his investments drop by 20% during a market correction stressful. So, while Sarah might be more willing to embrace volatility, Mark prefers stability and consistency.

One of the best ways to manage risk is to align your investments with your time horizon. If you're planning to invest for the long term, such as for retirement in 30 years, you might tolerate more risk early on, knowing that markets generally rise over the long term. However, as you approach your goal—say, within 5 to 10 years of retirement—you might want to start shifting your portfolio toward safer assets to protect the wealth you've built. For example, if you've accumulated a significant amount in stocks, you could gradually allocate a portion into bonds or other stable investments to reduce the overall risk.

This concept of adjusting risk based on time is often referred to as a "glide path." It's a strategy used by many investors, especially those saving for retirement, to gradually reduce exposure to riskier assets as their goals draw nearer.

Diversification: Don't Put All Your Eggs in One Basket

When you hear the phrase "Don't put all your eggs in one basket," it's a simple reminder of one of the most powerful strategies in investing: diversification. Diversification involves spreading your investments across different types of assets, industries, and even geographical regions to reduce risk. The idea is that if one investment performs poorly, others may perform better, which helps stabilize your overall portfolio.

Think of diversification as creating a well-rounded meal. If you eat only one type of food, you may end up with a nutrient deficiency. But by including a variety of foods—carbs, proteins, vegetables, and fruits—you ensure that you're getting a balanced, nutritious meal. Similarly, by diversifying your investments, you're ensuring that your financial health isn't overly reliant on one asset or market sector.

Consider the story of John, an investor who started by investing only in tech stocks. For a while, his portfolio was growing rapidly, thanks to the success of companies like Apple, Google, and Amazon. But when the tech bubble burst during a market correction, John saw a significant portion of his wealth evaporate. He quickly learned the importance of diversification. To balance his portfolio, John began investing in real estate, bonds, and even international stocks. By adding variety, he spread the risk across different asset classes, and his portfolio became much more resilient to market fluctuations.

Diversification doesn't mean you need to own hundreds of different stocks or investments. Many investors use mutual funds or exchange-traded funds (ETFs) to achieve diversification without the hassle of picking individual stocks. These funds pool together a wide range of assets, allowing you to invest in a broad array of companies, industries, and bonds with a single purchase. The key is to balance the risk and return across different types of investments to create a portfolio that works for you.

When it comes to diversifying your investments, consider the three main areas of diversification: asset class (stocks, bonds, real estate, etc.), sector (technology, healthcare, energy, etc.), and geography (domestic vs. international investments). By spreading your investments across these areas, you can reduce your overall risk and increase the potential for steady, long-term growth.

Starting Your Investment Plan

Getting started with investing can seem daunting, especially if you're new to the world of finance. But the truth is, that creating an investment plan doesn't have to be complicated. In this section, we'll break down the practical steps involved in starting your investment journey, beginning with budgeting for investments, building an emergency fund, and crafting a simple plan that aligns with your financial goals.

Budgeting for Investments: Analyzing Income and Expenses, Automating Savings, Budgeting with Investment Goals

Before you can start investing, it's important to understand where your money is currently going. A budget is the foundation of any financial plan. Think of it as the blueprint for your financial house. Without a clear understanding of your income and expenses, you might find it difficult to allocate funds for investing, or worse, run into financial difficulties down the road.

Start by analyzing your income and expenses. The first step in budgeting is to track your sources of income—your salary, freelance work, passive income, or any other sources of funds. Then, take a close look at your monthly expenses. Be honest with yourself: how much do you spend on essentials like rent, utilities, groceries, and transportation? What about non-essential spending on dining out, entertainment, or impulse buys? Keeping track of every dollar that comes in and out of your bank account will help you understand where you stand financially and how much you can realistically allocate to your investment goals.

Once you have a clear picture of your income and expenses, the next step is to automate your savings. Automation is key because it removes the temptation to spend money that should be invested. Set up automatic transfers from your checking account to a dedicated savings or investment account, ideally right after you get paid. This way, investing becomes a priority instead of an afterthought. Even if it's just a small amount—say $50 or $100 per month—it's better to start small and be consistent. Over time, these automated contributions will build up, helping you reach your investment goals.

But how do you know how much to save for investing? One strategy is to treat investing as a non-negotiable expense. Just as you would budget for rent, utilities, and groceries, allocate a specific percentage of your income for investments. Ideally, aim to invest 15-20% of your income. If that's too much to start with, you can begin with a smaller percentage and gradually increase it as your income grows or your expenses decrease.

For example, Sarah, a 30-year-old professional, started budgeting for investments by first tracking her monthly income and expenses. After reviewing her spending habits, she realized she was spending too much on eating out and subscription services she didn't use. She made a few adjustments and redirected that money into an investment account. She automated her savings, making sure that 15% of her monthly income was sent directly to her investment account. By doing this, she didn't have to think about it—her money was working for her while she focused on growing her career.

The key takeaway here is that budgeting is essential for building a solid foundation for investing. By automating savings and being intentional about how much you allocate, you'll set yourself up for success in the long term.

Building an Emergency Fund: Purpose of an Emergency Fund, How Much to Save, Ensuring Financial Security

Before diving into investing, it's crucial to have a financial safety net—an emergency fund. Think of your emergency fund as your financial buffer, providing you with peace of mind in case of unexpected events. Life is unpredictable, and having an emergency fund ensures that you won't need to tap into your investments or go into debt when something unexpected happens, such as a job loss, medical emergency, or major car repair.

So, how much should you save for an emergency fund? Financial experts typically recommend saving three to six months' worth of living expenses. This amount allows you to cover your basic needs, such as housing, utilities, food, and transportation, if something unexpected happens and you're unable to work. If your job is more volatile or you have a family to support, you may want to aim for a larger cushion—up to nine months' worth of expenses.

For example, David, a freelance graphic designer, decided to build an emergency fund before he started investing. He knew that as a freelancer, his income could fluctuate from month to month. After calculating his monthly expenses, he set a goal of saving $12,000—about six months' worth of living expenses. He created a separate savings account specifically for this fund and prioritized building it up before moving forward with investments. Once he had the funds in place, David felt more secure in his financial situation and was ready to start investing without the constant worry of what would happen if he faced an emergency.

Building an emergency fund takes time, but it's a vital step in ensuring your financial security. Start by setting small, manageable goals. Maybe your first target is $1,000, or maybe it's enough to cover one month of living expenses. Once you reach that goal, you can gradually build it up to the recommended three to six months of expenses. Keep in mind that your emergency fund should be liquid—meaning it should be easily accessible when you need it. Savings accounts, money market accounts, or short-term certificates of deposit (CDs) are ideal for emergency funds, as they offer low risk and easy access to your money.

Remember, the emergency fund is separate from your investment fund. The money you save for emergencies should not be invested in the stock market or other high-risk assets. It needs to be easily accessible and stable, so you can use it when the unexpected occurs without having to worry about market fluctuations.

Crafting a Simple Plan: Setting a Starting Capital Amount, Choosing Entry-Level Investments, Creating a Timeline

With your budget in place and an emergency fund set up, it's time to get serious about creating your investment plan. The first step is to decide how much capital you're going to start with. This amount will vary based on your financial situation, but the key is to start with what you're comfortable investing. It's essential to remember that investing doesn't require a large lump sum upfront. Even if you start with just a few hundred dollars, the important thing is to begin the process.

Setting a starting capital amount is a personal decision. For some, it may be $500, while for others, it might be $5,000. The key is to start small if you need to and then increase your contributions over time. It's better to start with a manageable amount and get comfortable with the process than to wait until you have a large sum to invest.

Once you've decided how much to invest, the next step is choosing your entry-level investments. If you're new to investing, it's important to keep things simple and focus on low-cost, diversified options. Index funds and exchange-traded funds (ETFs) are excellent entry points for beginners. These funds allow you to invest in a broad range of assets, which helps reduce risk while providing the growth potential. For example, a total market index fund will give you exposure to thousands of companies across different sectors, which helps spread out your risk.

Another option for beginners is target-date funds, which automatically adjust your portfolio based on your target retirement date. These funds gradually become more conservative as the target date approaches, making them a good choice for people who want a hands-off approach to investing.

Once you've chosen your investments, the final step is to create a timeline for your investment goals. Your timeline will depend on your financial objectives. Are you investing for a down payment on a house in five years? Or are you investing for retirement 30 years down the line? Knowing your time horizon is essential in determining the right mix of investments. The longer your timeline, the more you can afford to take on risk, knowing that you have time to recover from market fluctuations.

For example, Emily, a 28-year-old software engineer, decided to start investing for retirement. She set up a Roth IRA and allocated $200 per month to a diversified mix of index funds and ETFs. Her goal was to retire in 30 years, so she took a more aggressive approach to investing. Emily also set up an automatic transfer from her checking account to her investment account every payday, ensuring that she stayed on track with her timeline.

By crafting a simple, clear plan with starting capital, entry-level investments, and a realistic timeline, you create a roadmap for your financial future. This plan doesn't have to be set in stone; it can evolve as your financial situation changes. The key is to get started and make adjustments along the way.

Chapter 2: Safe Investment Options

Investing can be an exciting and potentially lucrative way to build wealth, but it's not without its risks. While many people associate investing with volatility and the possibility of losing money, there are safe investment options that allow you to grow your wealth without taking on excessive risk. In this section, we'll explore what invests "safe," the benefits of stability, and how to avoid common pitfalls that can hinder your financial growth.

Understanding Safe Investments

The term "safe investment" often refers to assets that are low in risk, where you're less likely to lose your principal— the original amount you invested. Safe investments typically provide predictable returns over time and are often used by investors who prefer stability and less volatility. However, just because an investment is considered "safe" doesn't mean it is entirely risk-free. All investments carry some level of risk, but safe investments minimize those risks while providing reasonable returns.

The most common characteristics of safe investments include low volatility, consistent returns, and a relatively low chance of losing your principal. These types of investments usually come from highly stable sources, such as government bonds, blue-chip stocks, or highly rated municipal bonds. These investments offer lower returns compared to more volatile options like individual stocks or cryptocurrencies, but they do so with the tradeoff of significantly reducing risk.

One of the most well-known examples of a safe investment is a **U.S. Treasury bond**. U.S. Treasuries are backed by the U.S. government, making them one of the safest investments available. They are considered low-risk because they are guaranteed by the government, and the return, while modest, is predictable. Investors who purchase Treasury bonds know that their money will grow steadily over time with minimal risk.

Another example of a safe investment is a **certificate of deposit (CD)**. Offered by banks, a CD allows you to deposit a sum of money for a fixed period at a guaranteed interest rate. While the return may be lower than that of stocks or mutual funds, your principal is safe, and you can count on earning predictable interest throughout the term. CDs are federally insured up to $250,000 per depositor, making them a particularly attractive option for conservative investors.

Finally, blue-chip stocks represent shares of well-established companies with a history of stable earnings and dividends. These are considered safer than smaller or newer companies, as they tend to be less volatile, and their performance is often more predictable. While investing in blue-chip stocks still carries some risk, they generally offer consistent returns and provide a degree of financial security compared to riskier investment options.

Balancing safety with returns is one of the key challenges of investing. A purely safe investment may not generate the high returns you hope for, but it can provide a foundation of stability upon which you can build more aggressive strategies. For example, investing a portion of your portfolio in government bonds or a diversified bond fund can offer predictable returns while you take on slightly more risk with other investments, like equities or real estate. Striking this balance is essential to achieving long-term financial success.

Benefits of Stability

Investing in safe assets can provide many benefits, especially if you're someone who values stability and peace of mind. One of the most significant advantages is **predictable returns**. Safe investments, like government bonds, blue-chip stocks, or high-quality corporate bonds, typically provide steady growth over time. Although they may not deliver the same explosive returns as more volatile assets, they offer consistency. This predictability allows investors to plan for the future with more confidence, knowing that their investments will grow at a reliable rate.

For example, consider Michael, a 40-year-old teacher who has been saving for retirement. Michael wants to invest but doesn't want to risk losing the money he's worked hard to accumulate. He decides to allocate a portion of his savings to U.S. Treasury bonds, which offer lower returns but come with little risk. As Michael approaches retirement, the steady and predictable growth of his bonds allows him to feel confident about his financial future. While his returns might not be as high as those of his friends who invested in riskier assets, Michael values the certainty that comes with safe investments.

Another major benefit of safe investments is **reduced emotional stress**. One of the most difficult aspects of investing in the stock market or more volatile assets is dealing with fluctuations. Watching your investments rise and fall can create anxiety, especially when the market experiences sharp drops. For conservative investors, the emotional toll of market volatility can be overwhelming. However, with safer investments, such as government bonds or well-established dividend-paying stocks, the stress of large swings in value is significantly reduced. Because safe investments tend to be less volatile, investors can focus on long-term growth rather than worrying about daily market fluctuations.

For example, Laura, an accountant in her early 50s, has a moderate risk tolerance. While she is open to some growth, she prefers to keep a large portion of her savings in safe investments to avoid the emotional stress that comes with more volatile markets. She invests in a mix of Treasury bonds, high-quality municipal bonds, and blue-chip stocks. By choosing these safe options, Laura doesn't stress about short-term market downturns, and instead, she feels secure in her long-term financial plan. The steady, predictable growth of her portfolio gives her peace of mind as she approaches retirement.

Perhaps the most valuable benefit of safe investments is the **financial peace of mind** they provide. Having a stable foundation allows you to weather economic storms without feeling like your financial future is at risk. In times of market downturns or financial crises, those who rely on safe investments tend to experience less anxiety. They can rest assured that their money is working for them, even if the broader market experiences volatility.

Take the example of Karen, a retiree in her late 60s who is living off of her savings. Karen remembers the 2008 financial crisis and how the stock market's sharp decline wiped out a significant portion of her portfolio. This time around, however, Karen took a more conservative approach. She invested a large portion of her savings into bonds and dividend-paying stocks. When the market dropped again, Karen didn't panic. While her portfolio was affected, the steady income from her bonds provided her with financial security. This allowed her to enjoy her retirement without the constant worry of losing everything in the stock market.

Avoiding Common Pitfalls

While safe investments offer stability and security, they are not without their own set of challenges. One of the most common mistakes that conservative investors make is being **overly cautious**. It's easy to think that sticking to the safest assets, like Treasury bonds or savings accounts, will always be the best choice. However, over time, these ultra-safe investments can result in underperformance due to inflation, which erodes the purchasing power of your money.

Consider the story of Peter, who decided to keep all his savings in a high-yield savings account. While he felt safe knowing his money was insured, he didn't account for the fact that inflation was steadily rising. Over a decade, Peter's savings account interest rate, while higher than average, wasn't enough to outpace inflation. As a result, the real value of his savings declined, and he was not able to purchase as much as he could have if he had diversified into other assets, such as stocks or real estate. In his case, playing it too safe ultimately led to a loss of purchasing power.

The lesson here is that while it's important to have safe investments, it's also essential to balance safety with growth potential. Keeping all your assets in low-return investments could limit your ability to achieve long-term financial goals. A diversified portfolio that includes a mix of safe investments, like bonds and dividend stocks, along with some higher-risk investments, can help protect you from the risk of inflation and allow your wealth to grow over time.

Another pitfall is **under-diversification**, or concentrating your investments in just one or two asset classes. While safe investments like Treasury bonds or blue-chip stocks are generally reliable, putting all your money into one category can expose you to risk. The value of a single asset class can be affected by factors beyond your control, such as changes in interest rates or company performance.

For example, Jack, a retired teacher, put nearly all his savings into high-quality municipal bonds, which he thought would provide the safest returns. While these bonds performed well for several years, the bond market took a hit when interest rates rose, causing the value of his bonds to decline. Had Jack diversified into a mix of bonds, dividend stocks, and perhaps some international investments, he could have better weathered the storm and minimized his losses.

The final pitfall to avoid is making **emotional decisions** based on short-term market fluctuations. Even with safe investments, there can be times when the market experiences volatility. During these moments, it's important to stick to your long-term plan and not panic. For example, if you own a mix of safe investments and the market experiences a downturn, don't sell everything in a rush just because you're worried about losing money. Emotional decisions, like selling during a market dip, can lock in losses and prevent you from benefiting from the recovery.

Linda, a conservative investor, faced a downturn in her bond holdings during the early months of the COVID-19 pandemic. Panicked, she considered selling her bonds to avoid further losses. However, after taking a step back and remembering her long-term goals, Linda decided to hold her position. Over time, her bonds recovered, and she was glad she didn't let her emotions dictate her decisions.

Low-Risk Investment Types

Investing can often feel overwhelming, especially when trying to balance risk with the desire for long-term financial growth. Fortunately, several low-risk investment types can provide steady returns with minimal volatility. These options offer safety while still providing growth opportunities. In this section, we'll explore three of the most popular low-risk investments: **bonds**, **dividend stocks**, and **money market funds & CDs**. We'll look at how they work, how they can be used in your investment strategy, and how to choose the right ones for your goals.

Bonds: Types of Bonds, Interest Rates, and How They Reduce Volatility

Bonds are one of the safest and most reliable ways to invest. A bond is essentially a loan that you give to a company or government entity in exchange for regular interest payments and the return of your principal at the end of the bond's term. There are several different types of bonds, and each offers different levels of risk, return, and security.

Types of Bonds

The two primary types of bonds are **government bonds** and **corporate bonds**.

1. **Government Bonds:** Government bonds are issued by national governments. They are considered some of the safest investments because they are backed by the full faith and credit of the government. For example, in the United States, **U.S. Treasury bonds** are known for their stability and safety. These bonds come with lower yields because of their lower risk, but they offer reliable, predictable returns. They are a good choice for investors who prioritize safety over high returns.
2. **Corporate Bonds:** Corporate bonds are issued by companies. The risk level here is higher than government bonds because companies can face financial difficulties that could affect their ability to repay the bonds. However, corporate bonds also offer higher yields as a reward for that additional risk. There are different credit ratings for corporate bonds (such as investment-grade or high-yield/junk bonds), which reflect the financial health of the issuing company. Choosing a reliable company with a strong credit rating can provide a balance between risk and return.

Interest Rates and Bond Prices

One of the most important aspects of investing in bonds is understanding how interest rates and bond prices are related. When interest rates rise, bond prices tend to fall, and when interest rates drop, bond prices generally rise. This inverse relationship exists because new bonds being issued at higher rates become more attractive than older bonds that offer lower rates. Conversely, if interest rates drop, older bonds with higher rates become more valuable.

The yield of a bond is the amount of interest it pays as a percentage of the current market price. For example, if you purchase a bond for $1,000 and it pays $50 in interest annually, the yield is 5%. If interest rates rise, bond prices fall, which means that older bonds offering lower interest rates become less attractive, thus reducing their price.

How Bonds Reduce Volatility

Bonds are generally less volatile than stocks, making them a great option for reducing overall portfolio risk. The predictable nature of bond interest payments helps investors avoid the emotional rollercoaster that often comes with the ups and downs of the stock market. For example, in times of market volatility or economic downturns, bonds tend to hold their value better than stocks, providing a stabilizing effect on your portfolio.

Bonds are also a great tool for investors who have a short- or medium-term investment horizon. Since bonds tend to be less volatile, they provide a stable source of income and are less likely to experience large fluctuations in price, making them a good option for conservative investors or those looking to reduce risk.

Dividend Stocks: Choosing Reliable Dividend Stocks, Reinvesting Dividends, and Creating Income

While stocks are generally considered riskier investments due to their volatility, **dividend-paying stocks** can offer a more stable option within the equity category. Dividend stocks are shares in companies that regularly distribute a portion of their earnings to shareholders, typically quarterly. These dividends are a source of income for investors, in addition to any potential capital gains from the increase in stock prices.

Choosing Reliable Dividend Stocks

The key to success in dividend investing is choosing reliable and consistent dividend-paying stocks. Not all companies pay dividends, and those that do may not be consistent in their payouts. When selecting dividend stocks, look for companies with a **long history** of paying dividends. These companies often have stable cash flows and a commitment to returning profits to shareholders.

Focus on **blue-chip stocks**—large, well-established companies with a history of steady earnings. These companies are more likely to weather economic downturns and continue to pay dividends. For example, consumer staples companies like Procter & Gamble or Johnson & Johnson, and utility companies like Duke Energy, have long histories of reliable dividend payouts.

It's also essential to pay attention to the **dividend yield**, which is the annual dividend divided by the stock's current price. A higher yield can seem attractive, but don't be swayed by extremely high dividend yields, as they may signal financial instability or that the company is struggling to maintain its dividend. Instead, aim for stocks with a moderate yield (generally between 2% to 6%) and a solid track record of increasing dividends over time.

Reinvesting Dividends

One of the most powerful ways to build wealth with dividend stocks is through **dividend reinvestment**. Instead of taking your dividend payouts in cash, you can choose to reinvest them to purchase more shares of the same stock. This strategy compounds your returns over time, as you begin to earn dividends on the additional shares you acquire through reinvestment.

Let's take a look at Sarah's strategy. She invested in a portfolio of dividend-paying stocks, including companies in the healthcare, technology, and consumer goods sectors. Rather than cashing out her quarterly dividends, she opted for a dividend reinvestment plan (DRIP). Over the course of several years, Sarah's reinvested dividends allowed her portfolio to grow significantly, as she acquired more shares without adding more capital. This strategy can be particularly powerful over long periods, as the compounding effect can dramatically increase the value of your investments.

Creating Income with Dividends

Dividend stocks are also an excellent option for those seeking **income** in retirement or as a supplement to their regular income. When you hold dividend-paying stocks in your portfolio, you can receive a regular stream of income from the dividends paid out by the companies. For example, if you own 1,000 shares of a company that pays $2 in dividends per share annually, you would receive $2,000 in dividend income each year.

Many retirees use dividend income as a primary source of cash flow, while still maintaining their stock holdings for long-term growth. By carefully selecting dividend stocks with reliable payouts and reinvesting dividends, you can build an income-generating portfolio that provides regular cash flow without selling your investments.

Money Market Funds and CDs: Advantages of Liquidity, Understanding CDs vs. Money Markets, and Using Them for Short-Term Goals

Both **money market funds** and **certificates of deposit (CDs)** are considered low-risk, liquid investments, making them ideal for short-term savings goals or for those looking to park their money safely for a while.

Advantages of Liquidity

Liquidity refers to how easily an investment can be converted into cash without significantly affecting its value. Money market funds and CDs offer relatively high liquidity compared to other investment types, making them a great choice if you anticipate needing access to your funds soon. While these investments are low-risk, they are also highly liquid, which means you can easily access your funds when necessary.

Money market funds, for instance, allow you to invest in a pool of short-term, high-quality debt securities, such as U.S. Treasury bills or certificates of deposit. They offer safety, as they invest in very low-risk assets, and provide liquidity since you can typically redeem your shares daily.

CDs, on the other hand, require you to commit your funds for a specified period, which can range from a few months to several years. In return for locking in your money for the agreed-upon term, you receive a fixed interest rate. While you cannot access your money without a penalty until the maturity date, CDs are a good choice for investors looking to earn higher interest rates than a savings account, without the risk of stock market fluctuations.

Understanding CDs vs. Money Markets

The main difference between money market funds and CDs lies in their structure and flexibility. Money market funds generally offer more liquidity and lower interest rates. However, they are still an attractive option for those looking for a safe place to park their funds temporarily. On the other hand, CDs provide a higher interest rate in exchange for locking your money away for a set period. The longer the term, the higher the interest rate you typically receive.

A money market fund is ideal for short-term goals where you may need to access your money quickly—such as saving for a vacation or an emergency fund. It offers the flexibility to withdraw funds at any time without penalties, though returns may be slightly lower than those offered by CDs. CDs are better suited for goals with a longer time horizon, where you won't need to access the funds before the maturity date, such as saving for a down payment on a house.

Using Them for Short-Term Goals

Money market funds and CDs are excellent for saving for **short-term financial goals**, such as an emergency fund, a car purchase, or a vacation. The low-risk nature of these investments makes them ideal for short-term savings, and their liquidity ensures that you can access your funds when you need them most.

For example, Emily is saving for a wedding that will take place in two years. She doesn't want to risk losing any of her money by investing it in the stock market, but she also wants to earn some interest while saving. She places her savings in a **money market fund** to keep her funds liquid and safe, earning a small but steady return. When the wedding day arrives, she can easily access the money without worrying about fluctuations in the market.

Strategies for Safe Returns

Achieving steady returns from safe investments requires more than just picking the right assets; it involves implementing strategies that help manage risk, maximize returns over time, and keep emotions out of the equation. In this section, we will dive into three powerful strategies for ensuring safe and consistent returns: **Dollar-Cost Averaging (DCA)**, **Reinvesting Dividends**, and **Building a Balanced Portfolio**. These approaches are designed to minimize risk while helping you build wealth over the long term.

Dollar-Cost Averaging (DCA): How DCA Minimizes Risk and Creates Consistency

One of the simplest and most effective strategies for investing safely is **Dollar-Cost Averaging (DCA)**. This strategy involves consistently investing a fixed amount of money into an asset, such as a stock or bond, at regular intervals, regardless of the asset's price. By sticking to this approach, you avoid trying to time the market, which can be difficult even for experienced investors.

How DCA Minimizes Risk

The primary benefit of DCA is that it helps to mitigate the risk of market fluctuations. Because you are investing a fixed amount regularly, you automatically buy more shares when prices are low and fewer shares when prices are high. This creates a "smoothing" effect, as it lowers your average cost per share over time, reducing the impact of volatility on your portfolio.

For instance, imagine you are investing $500 per month into a diversified fund. In some months, the market might be up, meaning your $500 buys fewer shares. In other months, when the market is down, your $500 buys more shares. Over time, this approach can help you avoid the risk of investing a lump sum just before a market downturn, which can be emotionally and financially devastating.

Creating a Consistent Habit

Another benefit of DCA is that it encourages **discipline and consistency**. Rather than worrying about market timing, you set up an automatic plan to invest a set amount regularly—whether the market is up or down. This consistent approach removes the emotional component of investing, which can often lead to poor decision-making. When you invest regularly, you are more likely to remain committed to your investment strategy, even when markets experience short-term turbulence.

A great example of the success of DCA is **Warren Buffett's** approach to investing. While he is known for making large, strategic investments, he also recommends DCA for individuals looking to build wealth steadily. He advocates for the regular investment of funds into low-cost index funds, which allows investors to benefit from the market's long-term growth without trying to predict short-term movements.

Examples of Long-Term DCA Success

DCA has been proven to be a successful strategy over time. A historical example involves an investor who began investing $1,000 per month into the **S&P 500 index** in 1990. By the time this investor retired in 2020, the portfolio would have grown significantly—despite numerous ups and downs in the market. The investor did not have to worry about timing the market or making major decisions during times of uncertainty. Instead, they consistently invested and allowed the power of long-term growth and compounding to work in their favor. Over decades, DCA has produced reliable growth, especially when invested in strong, diversified funds.

Reinvesting Dividends: Compounding with Dividends and Ideal Stocks for Reinvestment

Another critical strategy for safe returns is **reinvesting dividends**. Dividends are payments made by companies to shareholders as a portion of their profits. For long-term investors, **reinvesting dividends** can significantly enhance portfolio growth by allowing dividends to compound and generate additional income.

Compounding with Dividends

When you reinvest your dividends, you use the payouts to buy more shares of the same investment, thus **compounding** your returns. Each dividend payment adds more shares to your position, which then generates even more dividends in subsequent periods. Over time, this creates a snowball effect—what's known as the "compounding" effect—where your returns start to grow exponentially.

For example, consider you own 100 shares of a company that pays a $2 dividend per share annually. You would receive $200 in dividends. If you reinvest those dividends to buy more shares, your 100 shares will grow. In the next year, you will receive dividends on the additional shares, meaning your earnings will increase, and you'll be able to reinvest even more. This cycle continues, and the more shares you accumulate, the greater the growth potential. The longer you reinvest, the greater the cumulative impact, as your dividends generate further dividends, accelerating the compounding process.

Automatic Reinvestment Plans (DRIPs)
One of the easiest ways to reinvest dividends is by enrolling in a **Dividend Reinvestment Plan (DRIP)**. DRIPs are offered by many companies, allowing you to automatically reinvest your dividends into additional shares of the same stock, often without paying any commission fees. This option removes the need for manual intervention, ensuring that you're continuously growing your position without having to think about it.

For instance, if you invest in a company like **Coca-Cola** or **Johnson & Johnson**, which have long histories of reliable and growing dividends, you can choose to have those dividends reinvested automatically. Over time, this strategy can result in significant gains, especially if you stick to the plan for many years.

Ideal Stocks for Reinvestment

When selecting stocks to reinvest dividends, focus on companies with a **consistent track record of**

paying and increasing dividends. These are typically large, well-established companies with a proven ability to generate stable cash flow. Some examples include utility companies, consumer staples, and pharmaceutical giants.

However, be sure to evaluate the dividend **yield** and the company's financial health. A high dividend yield can seem attractive, but it's important to ensure that the company can sustain those dividends in the future. Investing in stocks with sustainable, growing dividends allows you to reap the benefits of compounding without worrying about the risk of dividend cuts.

For example, **Procter & Gamble** has a long history of steadily increasing its dividends, making it an excellent candidate for a DRIP strategy. Similarly, **PepsiCo** and **McDonald's** are known for their reliability and growth in both dividends and stock prices. These types of companies are often ideal choices for long-term dividend reinvestment strategies.

Building a Balanced Portfolio: Stocks and Bonds Allocation, Adjusting for Risk Tolerance, and Maintaining Diversification

One of the cornerstones of any safe investment strategy is maintaining a **balanced portfolio**. A balanced portfolio consists of a mixture of different asset classes—primarily stocks and bonds—that align with your investment goals, risk tolerance, and time horizon. The idea is to reduce risk while still positioning your investments for growth.

Stocks and Bonds Allocation

The foundation of a balanced portfolio is deciding the right proportion of stocks and bonds. Stocks are generally riskier but offer higher long-term growth potential, while bonds are more stable and provide steady, predictable income. A typical starting point for a balanced portfolio might be 60% stocks and 40% bonds. This allocation provides growth potential through stocks while mitigating risk with bonds.

However, your ideal allocation depends on your financial situation. For example, if you're younger and have a long investment horizon, you might lean more heavily toward stocks (such as an 80% stocks and 20% bonds allocation). Conversely, if you're nearing retirement or have a low-risk tolerance, you might favor more bonds, such as a 40% stocks and a 60% bonds split.

Adjusting for Risk Tolerance

Your **risk tolerance** plays a significant role in determining your portfolio allocation. Risk tolerance is a measure of how much volatility you're comfortable with in your investments. If you're someone who gets anxious during market downturns, a more conservative portfolio with a larger bond allocation might be the best choice. On the other hand, if you're comfortable with the ups and downs of the market and have a long-term view, you can afford to take more risk by increasing your stock allocation.

The key is to be honest with yourself about your risk tolerance and adjust your portfolio accordingly. As you age or your financial goals shift, you may choose to gradually reduce your exposure to riskier assets like stocks and increase your allocation to more conservative investments like bonds.

Maintaining a Diversified Mix

Diversification is another essential component of building a balanced portfolio. This means spreading your investments across a variety of asset classes, sectors, and geographic regions to reduce the risk of a major loss from any single investment. By diversifying, you protect yourself from downturns in specific sectors or industries and help smooth out the performance of your overall portfolio.

For example, instead of investing all your money in one or two companies, you can diversify by holding a variety of **stocks** across different sectors (technology, healthcare, consumer goods) and **bonds** (corporate bonds, government bonds). You can also consider international diversification by investing in global stocks or international bond markets. The more diverse your portfolio, the less likely a single market event will significantly harm your overall returns.

By keeping a balanced and diversified portfolio, you can manage risk more effectively while still positioning yourself for growth over the long term.

Chapter 3: Stock Market Fundamentals

What Are Stocks?

Stocks are one of the most popular investment choices, and for good reason. They offer the potential for high returns, allowing investors to benefit from the growth of companies and the broader economy. However, understanding stocks goes beyond simply buying a few shares. It's crucial to grasp what stocks represent, how their prices are determined, and how different types of stocks can fit into your investment strategy. This section will take you through the core concepts of stocks, their mechanics, and how you can use them to your advantage.

Ownership and Value: Defining Shares and How Stock Prices Are Determined

At their core, stocks represent **ownership** in a company. When you purchase a share of stock, you are buying a small piece of the company, becoming a **shareholder**. This means you own a portion of that company and are entitled to certain benefits, like receiving dividends or voting on important company decisions (depending on the type of stock you own).

Shares and Ownership

The number of shares in circulation represents the **equity** or ownership value of the company. A company might issue millions or even billions of shares, depending on its size. These shares are traded on the stock market, where investors can buy or sell them based on their view of the company's prospects. If the company performs well, its stock price will generally rise, and if it underperforms, its stock price will typically fall.

For example, imagine you own 100 shares of a company that has issued 10,000 shares in total. This means you own 1% of the company. If the company grows, your 1% ownership could increase in value, allowing you to sell those shares at a higher price than what you paid for them.

How Stock Prices Are Determined

Stock prices are determined by **supply and demand** in the market. If more people want to buy a stock than sell it, the price will rise, and if more people want to sell than buy, the price will fall. This dynamic is influenced by a range of factors, including:

1. **Company Performance**: Strong earnings reports, new product launches, or expansion into new markets can lead to a rise in stock prices as investors perceive the company's value to be increasing.
2. **Market Sentiment**: The broader economic environment or investor sentiment can influence stock prices. For instance, positive news in the economy or market might lead investors to buy stocks, pushing prices up.
3. **Industry Trends**: If an entire industry is doing well, individual companies within that sector may see their stock prices increase as well. Similarly, if a sector faces challenges, the companies within it may suffer.

For instance, during the tech boom of the late 1990s, companies like **Amazon** and **Microsoft** saw their stock prices soar as investors became excited about the potential of the internet and technology. Similarly, today's renewable energy boom has boosted the stock prices of companies in the solar and wind sectors.

Impact of Company Performance

The performance of the company is perhaps the most significant factor affecting stock prices. Strong

earnings reports—showing increased profits, revenue, or market share—typically drive stock prices higher. Conversely, if a company reports losses or misses analysts' expectations, its stock price may drop.

For example, when **Apple** reported record sales of the iPhone, its stock price surged. On the flip side, if a company experiences a scandal or financial trouble, such as a product recall or loss of a key executive, its stock price can fall dramatically.

Types of Stocks: Common vs. Preferred Stocks, Growth vs. Value Stocks, and Understanding Blue-Chip Stocks

There are several different types of stocks, each with its characteristics, benefits, and risks. Understanding these types of stocks can help you make more informed investment decisions based on your goals and risk tolerance.

Common vs. Preferred Stock

The two main types of stocks are **common stock** and **preferred stock**, each with different rights and privileges.

- **Common Stock**: As a holder of common stock, you have voting rights at the company's annual meeting and the potential to earn dividends. Common stockholders are last in line to be paid if the company goes bankrupt. However, they

have the potential for the highest rewards, as common stock usually offers more substantial price appreciation.
- **Preferred Stock**: Preferred stockholders typically do not have voting rights, but they are prioritized over common stockholders when it comes to dividend payments and in the event of bankruptcy. This type of stock is more stable and offers fixed dividends, which makes it attractive for conservative investors seeking regular income. However, the upside potential is typically limited compared to common stock, which is more volatile but can yield higher returns.

An example of this can be seen with **Tesla**. If you owned common stock in Tesla, you could vote in shareholder meetings, and your stock price would fluctuate more wildly. However, preferred stockholders would receive fixed dividends and would have less exposure to volatility.

Growth vs. Value Stock

Another important distinction in the world of stocks is between **growth stocks** and **value stocks**.

- **Growth Stocks** are shares in companies that are expected to grow at an above-average rate compared to other companies. These companies often reinvest their profits to fuel expansion rather than paying out dividends. Investors in growth stocks are usually looking for capital appreciation (increased share price) rather than income. **Amazon** and **Netflix** are classic examples of growth stocks, with investors willing to pay a premium for the expectation that these companies will continue to grow rapidly.

- **Value Stocks** are shares in companies that are undervalued relative to their earnings, often due to temporary issues that might be affecting the stock price. These stocks typically have lower price-to-earnings (P/E) ratios and may offer higher-than-average dividend yields. Value stocks appeal to investors who want to buy stocks at a discount, with the expectation that the market will eventually recognize the company's true value. **Ford** and **Johnson & Johnson** are examples of value stocks.

The choice between growth and value stocks depends largely on your investment goals. If you're seeking long-term growth and can tolerate short-term volatility, growth stocks might be a good choice. If you're looking for stability and steady income, value stocks could be more appropriate.

Blue-Chip Stocks

Another important category of stocks is **blue-chip stocks**. These are shares in large, well-established companies with a history of reliable performance, strong financials, and consistent dividend payments. **Apple**, **Microsoft**, **Coca-Cola**, and **Procter & Gamble** are all considered blue-chip stocks.

Blue-chip stocks are seen as less risky than smaller or newer companies, and they are often seen as a cornerstone of a well-diversified portfolio. These companies have proven their ability to weather market downturns and continue to thrive over time, making them a solid choice for long-term investors seeking stability.

Stock Market Mechanisms: Overview of Exchanges, Trading Hours, and Market Volatility

The stock market is a complex system with various components that come together to facilitate the buying and selling of shares. Understanding the mechanisms that drive stock exchanges and the factors influencing market volatility will help you navigate the market more effectively.

Overview of Exchanges

Stocks are bought and sold on exchanges, which are marketplaces that bring together buyers and sellers. The two largest stock exchanges in the world are the **New York Stock Exchange (NYSE)** and the **NASDAQ**. The NYSE is a physical exchange, where brokers trade stocks on a trading floor, while the NASDAQ is a fully electronic exchange.

Companies that want to raise capital by issuing stock will list their shares on one of these exchanges through a process called the **Initial Public Offering (IPO)**. Once listed, the shares are available for public trading, where investors can buy and sell them.

Exchanges provide transparency and regulation, ensuring that stock prices reflect the forces of supply and demand and that transactions are executed fairly. For investors, the exchange represents the platform on which they can trade their stocks.

Trading Hours and Market Factors

Stock markets operate during specific hours, with the NYSE and NASDAQ typically open from **9:30 a.m. to 4:00 p.m. EST** Monday through Friday. However, there is also **pre-market trading** and **after-hours trading**, during which stocks can be traded outside of regular market hours. These after-hours trades often experience more volatility, as fewer participants are involved.

Market factors that can affect stock prices include economic reports (like employment numbers), geopolitical events, and **interest rates**. For example, an unexpected **interest rate hike** by the Federal Reserve can lead to a market downturn, as it raises the cost of borrowing money and can reduce corporate profits.

Understanding Market Volatility

Market volatility refers to the degree of fluctuation in stock prices over time. **Volatile markets** are characterized by large price swings, and investors can experience both rapid gains and sharp losses. This is often seen in periods of economic uncertainty or global events, such as the **2008 financial crisis** or the market reaction to the **COVID-19 pandemic**.

While volatility presents a risk, it also presents opportunity for investors who are prepared. Understanding how to manage volatility—through diversification, staying invested for the long term, and avoiding emotional reactions—is key to navigating the ups and downs of the stock market.

Getting Started with Stocks

For many people, the idea of investing in stocks can be overwhelming, but the process is more straightforward than it may first appear. Whether you're aiming to build long-term wealth, create passive income, or simply expand your financial knowledge, understanding how to start with stocks is a critical step. In this section, we'll walk through the essentials of setting up a brokerage account, researching stocks, and embracing a solid buying-and-holding strategy.

Setting Up a Brokerage Account: Choosing a Platform, Understanding Fees, and Finding User-Friendly Options

Before you can begin purchasing stocks, you need to open a brokerage account. Think of it as a digital vault where your stocks are stored, and through which you can buy and sell them. There are numerous brokerage firms to choose from, each with different services, features, and pricing structures. Here's how to navigate the process.

Choosing a Platform

When selecting a brokerage account, it's important to assess your investing style and needs. Are you a hands-on investor who prefers making decisions on your own, or do you want access to expert advice and recommendations? Do you plan to trade frequently, or are you looking for a long-term investment vehicle? These questions can help guide your choice.

Online brokerage platforms like **Charles Schwab**, **Fidelity**, and **TD Ameritrade** are among the most well-known and trusted. They cater to both beginners and seasoned investors, providing easy-to-navigate interfaces and a variety of investment options. For those just starting, platforms like **Robinhood** and **Webull** also provide simple, commission-free trading with fewer features, which could be ideal if you are just dipping your toes into investing.

Some platforms also offer **robo-advisors**, such as **Betterment** or **Wealthfront**, which are ideal for those who don't have the time or expertise to manage their investments. These services use algorithms to create and manage a diversified portfolio based on your risk tolerance and financial goals.

Understanding Fees

When evaluating a brokerage, fees should be one of your top priorities. Some brokers charge commissions every time you buy or sell stocks, while others offer **commission-free trading**, meaning they don't charge for each trade. However, keep in mind that free trading often comes with other costs, such as fees for premium features or less favorable spreads between the buying and selling prices.

It's also important to understand **account maintenance fees**, which some platforms charge simply for having an account with them. Look for a brokerage with **no maintenance fees** or low-cost accounts to maximize your investment returns.

Finding User-Friendly Options

Especially for new investors, user-friendly platforms are critical. A simple, intuitive interface can make it much easier to navigate your portfolio, place trades, and access useful information about your investments. Check whether the platform offers **educational tools**, like tutorials, articles, or webinars, to help you get up to speed with the basics of investing.

Many brokers also offer **mobile apps**, so you can track your investments on the go. For example, platforms like **Fidelity** and **E*TRADE** allow you to manage your investments from your phone, which is especially helpful if you're a busy professional or just prefer using your mobile device.

Researching Stocks: Basics of Financial Ratios, Identifying Strong Companies, and Importance of Industry Research

Now that your account is set up, it's time to dive into researching stocks. The goal is to find solid companies that align with your investment strategy and offer the best chance for growth. While it's tempting to make decisions based on what's trending or the latest market buzz, conducting thorough research will help you make more informed decisions.

Basics of Financial Ratio

Financial ratios are essential tools for evaluating the health of a company. Here are a few key ratios that investors typically use:

- **Price-to-Earnings (P/E) Ratio**: The P/E ratio shows how much investors are willing to pay for each dollar of a company's earnings. A high P/E ratio can indicate that the company's stock is overvalued or that investors are expecting high growth in the future. A low P/E ratio may indicate that the stock is undervalued.

- **Earnings Per Share (EPS)**: EPS tells you how much profit a company is making on a per-share basis. A higher EPS often signals better profitability and operational efficiency.
- **Return on Equity (ROE)**: ROE measures a company's ability to generate profits from its shareholders' equity. A high ROE means the company is efficient at generating profits from its investments.
- **Debt-to-Equity Ratio (D/E)**: This ratio compares a company's total liabilities to its shareholders' equity. A high D/E ratio suggests that the company is heavily reliant on debt to finance its growth, which can be risky, particularly during market downturns.

By evaluating these ratios, you can assess a company's financial health and make more informed decisions about whether to invest. Tools like **Yahoo Finance**, **Morningstar**, or **Google Finance** allow you to easily access this information for most publicly traded companies.

Identifying Strong Companies

When researching potential stocks, it's essential to look for companies with a solid track record of success. Companies with strong revenue growth, robust cash flow, and effective management tend to weather economic challenges better than weaker competitors. Look for companies that operate in industries with long-term growth potential, such as technology, healthcare, or renewable energy.

Dividend-paying stocks are particularly appealing to investors who want to create passive income streams. Companies with a history of consistently paying dividends, such as **Coca-Cola** or **Johnson & Johnson**, tend to be more stable and less volatile, making them a great addition to a diversified portfolio.

For instance, if you're interested in investing in the technology sector, **Apple** and **Microsoft** have proven records of strong earnings and consistent growth. On the other hand, companies like **Procter & Gamble** or **PepsiCo** are staples in the consumer goods sector, providing stability and dividends.

Importance of Industry Research

Beyond looking at individual companies, it's crucial to understand the **industry** in which the company operates. For example, a company in the **technology** sector may offer significant growth potential, but it could also face increased competition and regulatory challenges. A company in **consumer staples**, like **Unilever**, may be more resilient during market downturns, as people still need to buy food, cleaning products, and other essentials.

Researching the broader industry helps you understand trends, competitive advantages, and potential risks. You can use industry reports from **IBISWorld**, **Statista**, and other data providers to get a clearer picture of how a company's industry is performing and whether it has long-term potential for growth.

Buying and Holding Strategy: Market Orders vs. Limit Orders, Benefits of Holding Long-Term, and Resisting Market Timing

Once you've identified stocks that align with your financial goals, the next step is buying those stocks. But how you execute your trades and your strategy for holding those stocks can significantly impact your long-term success.

Market Orders vs. Limit Order

When buying stocks, you can place two types of orders: **market orders** and **limit orders**.

- **Market Orders** are the simplest type of order. When you place a market order, you're agreeing to buy or sell the stock at the best available price at the time. Market orders are executed quickly, which is helpful if you want to buy or sell a stock immediately. However, there's a downside—if the stock is volatile or the market is moving quickly, you may not get the price you expect.
- **Limit Orders**, on the other hand, allow you to specify the price at which you're willing to buy or sell. For example, you could place a limit order to

buy a stock only if its price falls to a certain level. While limit orders give you more control over the price you pay, they may not always get executed if the stock doesn't reach your specified price.

For beginners, market orders are typically the simplest and quickest method, while limit orders are useful if you want to control your buying or selling price more precisely.

Benefits of Holding Long-Term

One of the key principles of investing is the **buy-and-hold** strategy. This means purchasing stocks with the intent of holding them for the long term—often years or decades. By holding onto quality stocks, you allow your investments to grow and compound over time.

The long-term approach works well because it allows you to take advantage of the **power of compounding**—where your returns earn returns. If you buy stocks in companies that are consistently growing and reinvest the dividends they pay, your portfolio can expand exponentially over time. A famous example of long-term success is **Warren Buffett**, who made billions by holding stocks for decades, letting compound interest do the heavy lifting.

Resisting Market Timing

Many new investors think they can outsmart the market by timing their buys and sells, but this is extremely difficult—even for the pros. The market is unpredictable, and trying to time it can lead to mistakes, such as buying when prices are high and selling when prices are low.

Instead of trying to time the market, focus on **consistency** and **long-term goals**. If you buy strong companies and hold them for years, you'll likely see significant gains despite the inevitable market fluctuations. History shows that, over time, the stock market tends to go up, even after periods of decline.

Avoiding Stock Market Mistakes

Investing in stocks can be highly rewarding, but it's easy to make mistakes that can derail your long-term financial goals. In this section, we'll explore some of the most common errors that new and even experienced investors make, and provide practical strategies for avoiding them. By understanding the pitfalls of overtrading, chasing trends, and panic selling, you can steer clear of these traps and stay on track to achieving financial independence.

Overtrading: Impact of Fees, Psychological Aspects, and Focusing on Long-Term Strategy

Overtrading occurs when investors buy and sell stocks too frequently, often with the belief that they can time the market or react to short-term market movements. While trading may seem exciting or even profitable in the short term, it's a strategy fraught with pitfalls that can damage your overall returns.

Impact of Fees

One of the immediate consequences of overtrading is the impact of **transaction fees**. Each time you buy or sell a stock, your brokerage charges a fee, which might seem small at first but can add up quickly if you're constantly making trades. For example, if your brokerage charges $5 per trade, and you make 100 trades a year, that's $500 in fees. For smaller portfolios, this amount can represent a significant portion of your returns, especially if the market isn't providing substantial growth in the short term.

Moreover, frequent trading might result in higher **tax liabilities**. In many countries, short-term capital gains (profits from assets held for less than a year) are taxed at higher rates than long-term capital gains, meaning that frequent traders are often hit with a higher tax bill.

Psychological Aspects of Overtrading

The psychological aspects of overtrading are just as dangerous as the financial ones. Many investors feel a psychological urge to act when they see their portfolio fluctuate. They may panic during a market dip, fearing they are losing money, or become overconfident during a market rally, thinking they can make quick profits. This emotional reaction to market movements is often the result of **short-term thinking**. Overtrading is typically fueled by **fear** or **greed**, two of the most powerful emotions that can cloud judgment.

The tendency to act impulsively in response to market fluctuations can be damaging to an investor's long-term success. For instance, during a downturn, an investor might panic-sell, only to regret the decision when the market rebounds. Conversely, during a bull market, they might become overly confident and take on too much risk.

Focusing on Long-Term Strategy

One of the best ways to avoid overtrading is to focus on a **long-term investment strategy**. Rather than reacting to every market swing, develop a plan based on your financial goals, risk tolerance, and investment horizon. A long-term strategy allows you to ride out market volatility without making rash decisions.

Investing with a long-term focus helps keep emotions in check and encourages patience. Successful investors like **Warren Buffett** have built their wealth by purchasing high-quality companies and holding them for many years, even decades. The strategy of buying and holding stocks for the long term—especially solid, dividend-paying stocks—can reduce the temptation to overtrade.

Chasing Trends: Risks of Following the Crowd, Importance of Research, and Sticking to Your Plan

Another common mistake is **chasing trends**—buying stocks based on what's popular or trending, rather than on sound research. It's tempting to follow the crowd, especially when everyone seems to be talking about a particular stock or sector. However, this approach is risky and often leads to poor outcomes.

Risks of Following the Crowd

The danger of chasing trends lies in the fact that stock prices can become detached from the fundamentals of a company. When a stock becomes "hot," its price might rise rapidly due to hype, not because of any underlying improvements in the company's performance or prospects. Investors who chase these stocks may be buying at inflated prices, which exposes them to the risk of a price correction or even a sharp decline.

Take the **Dot-com Bubble** of the late 1990s, for example. Many investors were caught up in the frenzy surrounding internet stocks, and as a result, stocks like **Pets.com** were trading at astronomical prices, despite not having a viable business model. When the bubble burst, many of these companies crashed, leaving investors with significant losses. Chasing the latest trend, without considering the fundamentals, can lead to buying stocks at their peak price—just before they begin to fall.

Importance of Research

Rather than simply following the crowd, it's essential to conduct your **research** before purchasing stocks. Start by evaluating a company's **financial health**, its track record, its management, and its industry prospects. You can use key financial metrics like the **price-to-earnings (P/E) ratio**, **earnings-per-share (EPS)**, and **return on equity (ROE)** to understand whether the company is a good investment.

Additionally, look beyond individual companies and consider the **industry** in which they operate. Some sectors may be overvalued or facing headwinds that could affect their growth prospects, while others may have long-term growth potential. Investing in companies within **stable industries** (e.g., consumer goods, healthcare) can reduce your risk and provide a more predictable path to success.

By sticking to thorough research and focusing on companies with strong fundamentals, you can avoid getting swept up in short-term trends that don't align with your long-term goals. Investing with a well-informed, data-driven mindset is far more likely to lead to sustainable growth than riding the wave of the latest market fad.

Sticking to Your Plan

One of the best ways to avoid chasing trends is to stick to your investment plan. When you create a plan based on your risk tolerance and financial goals, you have a roadmap that keeps you focused. This plan should be flexible enough to adjust for changes in your life or market conditions, but it should remain centered around the big picture.

If you find yourself tempted by the latest market trend, take a step back and ask whether it fits into your overall strategy. If it doesn't align with your goals or risk tolerance, resist the urge to jump in. A disciplined approach will help you avoid the costly mistakes that come from chasing trends without thinking about your long-term objectives.

Panic Selling: Avoiding Emotional Reactions, Strategies for Market Downturns, and Staying Calm and Rational

Panic selling is another mistake that can be detrimental to your long-term investment success. This occurs when investors sell off their stocks in response to short-term market volatility, often driven by fear and emotions.

Avoiding Emotional Reactions

The stock market is volatile, and prices fluctuate constantly. While it's natural to feel anxiety or fear when the market drops, making decisions based on these emotions is a surefire way to lose money. The key to avoiding panic selling is to understand that market downturns are a natural part of the investment cycle. Every market experiences ups and downs; it's how you respond to those fluctuations that will determine your success.

When you panic-sell, you're locking in your losses, which means you've effectively realized that you lost money. Instead of selling in response to a downturn, take a step back and evaluate the situation rationally. Ask yourself if the reasons you bought the stock still hold. If the company is still fundamentally strong and the market drop is simply a temporary fluctuation, then selling may be an overreaction.

Strategies for Market Downturns

During market downturns, one of the most effective strategies is to **stay the course**. Remember that stock markets tend to rise over the long term, even after periods of decline. The key is to avoid making knee-jerk reactions based on short-term volatility. If your investment strategy is built for the long haul, the short-term fluctuations won't matter in the grand scheme of things.

Another strategy to consider during downturns is **dollar-cost averaging (DCA)**. DCA involves investing a fixed amount of money at regular intervals, regardless of the market's direction. This strategy helps reduce the impact of market volatility because you're buying more shares when prices are low and fewer shares when prices are high. Over time, this approach smooths out the market's ups and downs and ensures that you stay invested consistently.

Staying Calm and Rational

Finally, staying calm and rational is critical during times of market uncertainty. Having a long-term perspective helps you weather the storm and avoid emotional reactions. Remind yourself of your goals, your strategy, and why you're investing in the first place. Taking a step back, analyzing your portfolio, and speaking with a financial advisor can also help you maintain perspective and avoid making decisions out of fear.

Chapter 4: Mutual Funds and ETFs

Understanding Mutual Funds

When you begin your investment journey, the vast range of options can be overwhelming. You might find yourself wondering whether individual stocks, bonds, or other vehicles like mutual funds or exchange-traded funds (ETFs) are the best choice. This section will focus on mutual funds, a popular investment option that can be especially beneficial for beginners. We will break down the basics, discuss the advantages of mutual funds for new investors, and explore key factors to consider when choosing one.

Basics of Mutual Funds: Pooling Investments, Active vs. Passive Funds, and the Role of Fund Managers

At their core, mutual funds are investment vehicles that pool money from many investors to invest in a diversified portfolio of assets, such as stocks, bonds, or other securities. Each investor owns a portion of the total fund, represented by shares of the mutual fund. By pooling investments, mutual funds provide smaller investors with access to a broader range of assets than they could typically afford on their own.

Pooling Investments

The primary appeal of mutual funds lies in their ability to combine resources from multiple investors. This pooling effect allows individual investors to hold shares in a wide variety of stocks, bonds, and other securities within a single investment. For example, a typical mutual fund might hold hundreds of different stocks across multiple industries, helping to diversify your exposure.

This diversification reduces the risk inherent in investing in individual stocks. By spreading your investments across many different assets, the negative performance of one stock may be offset by the positive performance of others. This helps to minimize the overall volatility of your investment, which is especially valuable if you are new to investing and prefer lower levels of risk.

Active vs. Passive Funds

Mutual funds are generally categorized into two types: **active** and **passive**.

- **Active Funds**: These funds are managed by professional portfolio managers who make decisions about which securities to buy and sell in order to outperform the market. Active fund managers rely on research, analysis, and their expertise to identify opportunities for higher returns. Because of the hands-on management required, active funds typically charge higher fees than passive funds.
- **Passive Funds**: Also known as **index funds**, these funds aim to replicate the performance of a specific market index, such as the **S&P 500**. Passive funds do not attempt to beat the market; instead, they aim to mirror the performance of an index by investing in the same stocks or bonds that are included in that index. Because passive funds do not require active management, their fees tend to be lower than those of actively managed funds.

The choice between active and passive funds often depends on your investment strategy and goals. If you're looking for higher potential returns and are willing to pay higher fees for the expertise of a professional fund manager, an active fund might be right for you. If you prefer lower fees and are content with market returns, a passive index fund may be more appealing.

The Role of Fund Managers

Fund managers play a crucial role in active mutual funds. These professionals are responsible for selecting the securities within the fund's portfolio. Their job is to analyze market trends, evaluate individual stocks and bonds, and make buy or sell decisions based on their analysis. Because of their expertise and experience, fund managers can provide valuable insight, potentially helping the fund outperform the broader market. However, it's important to note that not all fund managers are successful at consistently beating the market.

In passive funds, the role of a fund manager is far less hands-on. The goal of these funds is not to outperform the market but to track an index. Managers of index funds typically follow a pre-determined set of rules for investment, which helps maintain low costs and reduces the risk of human error.

Benefits for Beginners: Diversification in a Single Purchase, Accessibility, and Simplicity, and Reduced Individual Stock Risk

Mutual funds offer several advantages that make them especially attractive to new investors who may not have the time, resources, or expertise to select individual stocks or bonds.

Diversification in a Single Purchase

One of the most significant benefits of mutual funds is **diversification**. When you buy shares in a mutual fund, you are effectively buying into a diverse portfolio of assets. This diversification helps spread risk. For example, if you were to buy shares in a stock of a single company and that company's stock value plummeted, your entire investment would take a hit. In contrast, a mutual fund may hold a wide range of stocks, so even if one or two companies perform poorly, the overall fund may still perform well due to the strength of other assets.

For beginners, building a diversified portfolio by purchasing individual stocks can be daunting and expensive. With mutual funds, you can gain exposure to a wide array of assets for a relatively small initial investment, which provides significant risk reduction with just a single purchase.

Accessibility and Simplicity

Mutual funds are also highly **accessible** and **easy to understand**, which makes them a great choice for beginner investors. Unlike individual stocks, which require careful research into company performance, industry conditions, and market trends, mutual funds provide a more hands-off approach. All you need to do is choose a fund that aligns with your investment goals and risk tolerance.

Additionally, many mutual funds have low **minimum investment requirements**, which makes them accessible to most investors, even those just starting out. Some mutual funds may allow you to start investing with as little as $50 or $100, making them a more feasible option than trying to build a diversified portfolio of individual stocks with the same amount.

Reduced Individual Stock Risk

When you invest in individual stocks, you are exposed to the specific risks of the companies in which you invest. If one of those companies faces challenges—whether financial, operational, or industry-wide—your investment could be significantly impacted. However, mutual funds reduce this risk by holding a range of different securities. For example, an equity mutual fund might own shares in dozens or even hundreds of different companies. This helps protect your investment from the poor performance of any single stock.

Moreover, mutual funds also allow you to invest in different types of assets. A balanced mutual fund might invest in a mix of stocks and bonds, for example, which adds a layer of diversification.

Choosing a Mutual Fund: Factors to Consider (Fees, Performance), Types of Funds, and Aligning with Goals

While mutual funds are a great option for many investors, it's important to choose the right fund for your specific goals and needs. Several factors should be taken into account when selecting a mutual fund, including its fees, past performance, and the type of fund.

Factors to Consider (Fees, Performance)

- **Fees**: Fees are one of the most important factors to consider when choosing a mutual fund. Fees can eat into your returns over time, especially if you hold the fund for many years. There are several types of fees to be aware of:
    - **Expense ratio**: This annual fee is expressed as a percentage of the fund's assets. It covers the costs of managing the fund, such as salaries for fund managers, marketing, and operational expenses. Generally, actively managed funds have higher expense ratios than passive funds.

- ○ **Sales charges (loads)**: Some mutual funds charge a sales load when you buy or sell shares. These fees can be substantial, so it's essential to check for any upfront or back-end charges before investing.
- **Past performance**: While past performance does not guarantee future results, reviewing how a mutual fund has performed historically can provide insight into how it has managed risk and navigated market cycles. Look at the fund's long-term performance rather than short-term gains. Compare its performance to similar funds or relevant benchmarks to see if it has outperformed its peers.

However, it's crucial to remember that performance is not the only consideration. A fund that has performed well in the past might not continue to do so, especially if its management or strategy changes.

Types of Funds

There are several types of mutual funds to choose from, depending on your investment objectives:

- **Equity funds**: These funds invest in stocks and are ideal for investors seeking higher growth potential. They can be further categorized into large-cap, mid-cap, and small-cap funds, based on the size of the companies they invest in.

- **Bond funds**: These funds invest primarily in bonds and are a good choice for more conservative investors who want to reduce risk and focus on steady income.
- **Balanced funds**: These funds invest in both stocks and bonds, providing a balanced approach that can offer growth and income while managing risk.
- **Index funds**: These passive funds aim to replicate the performance of a specific market index, such as the **S&P 500**, and usually have lower fees than actively managed funds.

Aligning with Your Goals

Finally, when choosing a mutual fund, it's important to align the fund's characteristics with your personal **financial goals**. For example, if you are saving for retirement and have a long time horizon, you might choose an equity fund with high growth potential. If you are investing for a short-term goal, like buying a home, you might consider a bond fund for its stability and income generation.

Consider factors like your risk tolerance, investment time frame, and return expectations when selecting a fund. Some funds are better suited for aggressive growth, while others are designed for conservative income. Understanding your goals and risk tolerance will help you pick the fund that fits your needs.

Exploring ETFs

Exchange-Traded Funds (ETFs) have grown in popularity over the last two decades as an accessible and versatile investment option. With their ability to offer the diversification of mutual funds and the flexibility of individual stocks, ETFs have become a favorite for many investors, both novice and experienced. In this section, we will explore the basics of ETFs, compare them to mutual funds, and offer practical advice on how to select the right ETF based on your goals, risk tolerance, and financial objectives.

ETF Basics: How ETFs Work, Benefits of Trading Flexibility, and Examples of Popular ETFs

How ETFs Work

An ETF is a type of investment fund that holds a collection of assets, such as stocks, bonds, commodities, or other securities and trades on an exchange, much like individual stocks. When you invest in an ETF, you are essentially buying a small portion of the entire portfolio of assets the fund holds. For example, an ETF might track the **S&P 500**, a stock market index made up of 500 large companies, or it could focus on a specific sector like **technology** or **healthcare**.

ETFs are **passively managed** for the most part, especially those that track specific indexes, but there are also actively managed ETFs. In passive ETFs, fund managers select securities based on predefined rules, typically aiming to replicate the performance of a specific index rather than outperform it. This makes ETFs a popular choice for investors seeking lower management fees compared to actively managed funds.

Benefits of Trading Flexibility

One of the key benefits of ETFs is their **flexibility**. Unlike mutual funds, which are bought or sold at the end of the trading day at the net asset value (NAV), ETFs trade on the open market throughout the day, just like stocks. This means that you can buy and sell ETFs at any point during the market's trading hours, which gives investors more control over the timing of their transactions.

Additionally, the **intraday pricing** of ETFs provides transparency. You can monitor the price of an ETF throughout the day, ensuring that you're making purchases or sales at prices that reflect the most up-to-date market conditions. This level of flexibility allows for more precise control over the timing of your trades, especially if you're looking to take advantage of short-term market movements or make adjustments to your portfolio quickly.

Another advantage of ETFs over mutual funds is their **lower minimum investment** requirements. Most mutual funds require a minimum investment, which can range from a few hundred to thousands of dollars. ETFs, on the other hand, can be purchased in increments of a single share, making them more accessible for investors with smaller amounts to invest.

Examples of Popular ETFs

There are thousands of ETFs available, each designed to meet different investment objectives. Some of the most popular types of ETFs include:

- **Index ETFs**: These ETFs track major market indices, such as the **S&P 500** or the **NASDAQ-100**, offering broad exposure to large companies in the U.S. stock market. The **SPDR S&P 500 ETF (SPY)** and the **Vanguard Total Stock Market ETF (VTI)** are two examples of popular index ETFs.
- **Sector ETFs**: These ETFs target specific sectors of the economy, such as **technology**, **healthcare**, or **energy**. For instance, the **Technology Select Sector SPDR ETF (XLK)** focuses on technology stocks, while the **Health Care Select Sector SPDR ETF (XLV)** targets healthcare companies.
- **Bond ETFs**: For those seeking more conservative investments, bond ETFs provide exposure to fixed-income securities. Examples include the **iShares iBoxx $ Investment Grade Corporate Bond ETF (LQD)**, which holds investment-grade corporate bonds, or the **Vanguard Total Bond Market ETF (BND)**,

which includes a mix of U.S. government and corporate bonds.
- **International ETFs**: These ETFs focus on stocks or bonds outside of the U.S., providing exposure to global markets. The **Vanguard FTSE All-World ex-US ETF (VEU)** is an example of a global equity ETF that excludes U.S. companies.

These examples illustrate just how diverse ETFs can be, allowing investors to tailor their portfolios to suit specific sectors, geographic areas, or asset classes.

ETFs vs. Mutual Funds: Key Differences, When to Choose Each, and Understanding Costs and Tax Benefits

While both ETFs and mutual funds offer a diversified approach to investing, several key differences can influence your choice between the two. Understanding these differences is crucial for making an informed decision that aligns with your investment goals.

Key Differences Between ETFs and Mutual Funds

- **Trading Flexibility**: As mentioned earlier, one of the primary differences between ETFs and mutual funds is how they trade. ETFs trade on an exchange like a stock, with prices fluctuating throughout the day. Mutual funds, on the other hand, are priced once per day at the **net asset value (NAV)** after the market closes. This means

that with ETFs, you have more control over the timing of your trades, while mutual funds execute orders at the end of the day.
- **Management Style**: While both ETFs and mutual funds can be either actively or passively managed, the majority of ETFs are passively managed, especially those that track broad market indices. In contrast, many mutual funds are actively managed, which means fund managers are making decisions about which securities to buy or sell. Actively managed funds typically have higher fees because of the research and management involved.
- **Fees**: ETFs generally have lower fees than mutual funds. This is because most ETFs are passively managed, and the costs associated with managing them are relatively low. Mutual funds, especially actively managed ones, tend to have higher management fees due to the involvement of fund managers. This can make a big difference over time, especially if you're a long-term investor.
- **Minimum Investment**: Mutual funds often have minimum investment requirements, which can be a barrier for some investors. ETFs, on the other hand, can be bought in increments of a single share, making them more accessible for those with smaller amounts to invest.
- **Tax Efficiency**: ETFs tend to be more **tax-efficient** than mutual funds. This is because of the way they are structured. When you sell

shares of an ETF, you do so in the secondary market, rather than through the fund itself. This minimizes capital gains distributions, which can trigger taxes for mutual fund investors. In mutual funds, investors may receive capital gains distributions when the fund manager sells securities within the fund. However, with ETFs, there is no requirement for investors to sell their shares back to the fund, and as a result, there are fewer taxable events.

When to Choose ETFs or Mutual Funds

Both ETFs and mutual funds can play important roles in an investment portfolio. The choice between the two largely depends on your individual goals, investment style, and preferences.

- **Choose ETFs** if you prefer flexibility and lower costs. ETFs are ideal for investors who want to trade during market hours, take advantage of intraday price movements, or keep management fees to a minimum. They are also well-suited for investors who want to focus on passive investing or want to easily diversify across sectors or asset classes.
- **Choose Mutual Funds** if you are looking for professional management and are willing to pay higher fees for active decision-making. Mutual funds may be a better choice for investors who are not interested in managing their own

investments or who prefer a more hands-off approach. They can be a good option for retirement savings, where a long-term, buy-and-hold strategy is often the most effective.

Selecting an ETF: Evaluating ETFs by Sector, Researching Expense Ratios, and Aligning with Risk Tolerance

When selecting an ETF, it's essential to carefully evaluate your options based on your investment goals, risk tolerance, and the fund's structure.

Evaluating ETFs by Sector

Many ETFs are designed to target specific sectors or industries. If you want to gain exposure to a particular part of the market, sector ETFs can be an excellent option. For example, if you're bullish on the future of technology, you might choose a **technology ETF**. If you believe that energy companies will perform well in the coming years, an **energy sector ETF** could be a good fit.

Evaluating sector-specific ETFs involves understanding the performance and outlook of the industry. For instance, technology ETFs tend to do well when innovation is booming, but they can also be more volatile due to the rapid pace of change in the sector. On the other hand, ETFs focused on consumer staples or healthcare might be more stable, but with slower growth.

Researching Expense Ratios

Just like with mutual funds, ETFs come with expense ratios, which represent the annual fee for managing the fund. Lower expense ratios are generally better, as high fees can erode your returns over time. When comparing ETFs, make sure to pay close attention to the expense ratio and understand how it fits with your investment strategy. A high expense ratio might make sense for an actively managed ETF if you believe the manager will deliver strong returns, but for most investors, a low-cost passive ETF is often a better choice.

Aligning with Risk Tolerance

Finally, when selecting an ETF, you should always consider your risk tolerance. Some ETFs are designed to be more conservative, investing in bonds or stable blue-chip stocks, while others focus on higher-growth sectors, such as technology or emerging markets. It's important to select ETFs that align with your risk tolerance and investment horizon.

If you're young and have a long time to invest, you may be comfortable taking on more risk with sector ETFs or growth-focused ETFs. But if you're nearing retirement or need more stability, you might prefer ETFs that focus on bonds or dividend-paying stocks.

Managing Fund Investments

Managing investments in mutual funds and ETFs is a crucial aspect of any long-term investment strategy. After selecting the right funds for your goals, it's important to have a solid approach to managing them, ensuring they stay aligned with your financial objectives. This section will discuss three key strategies for managing fund investments: **dollar-cost averaging**, **rebalancing your portfolio**, and **evaluating performance**. By understanding how each of these strategies works, you can take a more active role in managing your portfolio and positioning yourself for success.

Dollar-Cost Averaging with Funds: Benefits of Steady Investments, Examples for Mutual Funds and ETFs, Risk Reduction

What is Dollar-Cost Averaging?

Dollar-cost averaging (DCA) is a strategy where an investor consistently invests a fixed amount of money at regular intervals, regardless of market conditions. This approach is particularly useful for long-term investors looking to reduce the impact of short-term market fluctuations. By investing the same amount regularly, you purchase more shares when prices are low and fewer shares when prices are high, averaging out the cost over time.

This method can be particularly effective when applied to both **mutual funds** and **ETFs**, as it helps you avoid the emotional and psychological pitfalls of trying to time the market. Market timing—attempting to predict the best times to buy and sell—can lead to poor investment decisions, especially for novice investors. DCA offers a more methodical, disciplined approach that encourages long-term growth without the worry of short-term market volatility.

Benefits of Dollar-Cost Averaging

The most obvious benefit of DCA is that it reduces the risk of making large investments during market peaks. Without DCA, investors may get caught up in the excitement during a bull market and invest large sums of money just before the market corrects. By using DCA, you spread out your risk over time, making it less likely that you'll purchase too much at an elevated price.

In addition, DCA reduces the emotional stress that often comes with investing. Markets can be volatile, and during periods of sharp declines, it's natural to feel anxious. With DCA, you're less likely to make knee-jerk reactions because you know your investments are being made consistently, without the need to monitor daily market movements.

Example with Mutual Funds and ETFs

Let's say you've chosen a **Vanguard Total Stock Market ETF (VTI)** for your portfolio, and you decide to invest $500 each month. No matter what the market is doing, you invest that same amount on the same day each month. In some months, the ETF's price might be higher, and in other months, it might be lower. Over time, however, the average cost of your shares will even out, reducing the risk of making a poorly timed investment.

For mutual funds, you can apply the same strategy. For example, if you invest $500 every month into a **Fidelity 500 Index Fund (FXAIX)**, the consistent, automatic purchases ensure you are buying shares at varying prices, giving you a smoother overall cost base. This is particularly helpful in volatile markets or when you don't have the time or expertise to follow the market closely.

In both cases, DCA helps to smooth out returns, making it a less stressful way to build wealth over the long term.

Rebalancing Your Portfolio: When and How to Rebalance, Importance of Alignment with Goals, Making Adjustments

What is Rebalancing?

Rebalancing refers to the process of adjusting the asset allocation of your portfolio to ensure that it remains aligned with your long-term goals, risk tolerance, and investment strategy. Over time, certain investments may outperform others, causing your portfolio to drift away from its original allocation. For instance, if you initially set your portfolio to be 60%

stocks and 40% bonds, but the stock portion grows faster than expected, you may end up with 70% stocks and 30% bonds. If left unchecked, this could result in a portfolio that no longer matches your risk profile.

Rebalancing involves selling some of the investments that have been appreciated and buying more of those that have underperformed, bringing your portfolio back into balance. It's a disciplined approach to maintain the risk-reward profile you originally set, ensuring that you're not taking on too much risk or being overly conservative.

When and How to Rebalance

Rebalancing is generally done **periodically**, either on a set schedule (e.g., annually or quarterly) or when the asset allocation deviates by a certain percentage (e.g., when a sector or asset class exceeds or falls below 5% of your target allocation). The most straightforward method is to review your portfolio once a year and make necessary adjustments. For example, if the stock portion of your portfolio grows beyond 60% due to a bull market, you would sell some stocks and purchase more bonds to return to your original target allocation.

However, rebalancing too often can result in unnecessary trading costs and taxes. It's important to strike the right balance—rebalancing often enough to maintain alignment with your goals but not so frequently that the process becomes counterproductive.

The Importance of Alignment with Goals

Rebalancing is not just about maintaining a specific asset allocation; it's also about ensuring that your portfolio continues to align with your evolving financial goals. If you've experienced a significant life event, such as a change in your career, a large financial windfall, or approaching retirement, you may need to adjust your portfolio to reflect these new circumstances. For example, if you're five years away from retirement, you may want to reduce the risk in your portfolio by shifting from growth-focused investments (like stocks) to more conservative ones (like bonds).

By revisiting your goals regularly, you can ensure that your portfolio remains aligned with your desired financial outcomes, such as funding a child's education, buying a home, or maintaining a comfortable lifestyle in retirement.

Making Adjustments

The process of rebalancing isn't always just about selling one asset and buying another. Sometimes, it might make more sense to make **strategic adjustments** to your holdings. For example, if your bond allocation is underperforming and you no longer find bonds appealing due to low interest rates, you might consider switching some of that allocation into a different asset class, such as dividend-paying stocks or real estate funds.

When rebalancing, it's essential to consider your tax situation, especially if your investments are in a taxable account. Selling investments can trigger capital gains taxes, so it's important to rebalance strategically. For instance, you might want to sell investments that have lost value, as those can offset capital gains and reduce your tax liability.

Evaluating Performance: Understanding Fund Returns, Comparing to Benchmarks, Deciding When to Stay or Switch

Understanding Fund Returns

Evaluating the performance of your investments is an essential part of managing a portfolio. Mutual funds and ETFs report returns regularly, typically monthly or quarterly, which reflect how much the fund's value has changed over that time. Returns are usually expressed as a **percentage**, so if a fund has returned 5% over the past year, that means your investment would have grown by 5%.

It's important to look at both **absolute returns** (the total return of the fund) and **relative returns** (how the fund has performed compared to a benchmark or similar funds). Returns can vary greatly from year to year, and past performance is not necessarily indicative of future results. However, consistent, positive returns over the long term are typically a good indicator that a fund is well-managed and has the potential to continue growing.

Comparing to Benchmarks

One of the most effective ways to evaluate a fund's performance is to compare it to a relevant **benchmark**. A benchmark is a standard used to measure how well the fund has performed relative to the broader market or a specific sector. For example, if you're invested in a large-cap equity fund, you might compare its returns to the **S&P 500**, which is a common benchmark for large-cap stocks. If your fund has consistently outperformed the S&P 500, it might indicate strong management or favorable market conditions.

In contrast, if your fund has underperformed its benchmark over a long period, it may suggest that the fund is not performing as expected. However, it's essential to consider **market conditions** before making a decision based solely on past performance. A fund might underperform in certain market conditions but do well when the economic environment changes.

Deciding When to Stay or Switch

Evaluating whether to stay in a fund or switch to another requires a careful assessment of the fund's past performance, fees, and alignment with your financial goals. If a fund has underperformed its benchmark consistently, or if it no longer fits your risk tolerance or objectives, it may be time to consider alternative investments.

However, it's important to avoid making knee-jerk decisions based on short-term performance. The stock market and investment funds are inherently volatile, and short-term underperformance is normal. Rather than making hasty decisions, it's better to have a long-term mindset and consider whether the fund still fits within your overall strategy.

When switching funds, always consider the **tax implications** and transaction costs. For example, selling a fund with gains may trigger capital gains taxes, which can eat into your returns. In addition, frequent trading can result in higher transaction fees, especially for mutual funds, which may have sales loads or commissions.

Chapter 5: Basics of Retirement Accounts

Types of Accounts, Tax Advantages, and Contribution Limits

Planning for retirement is a critical part of financial health, and understanding the different retirement account options is essential for building a secure future. Retirement accounts like IRAs, Roth IRAs, and 401(k) plans offer powerful benefits, including tax advantages that can significantly grow your wealth over time. However, each type of account has specific rules, limits, and benefits that are important to know so you can maximize your contributions and take advantage of tax benefits. In this section, we'll explore the types of accounts available, how they provide tax advantages, and how to make the most of your contributions.

Types of Accounts: IRA, Roth IRA, 401(k)

IRA (Individual Retirement Account)

An IRA, or Individual Retirement Account, is a popular retirement savings tool that allows individuals to set aside money with certain tax benefits. Traditional IRAs allow contributions to be tax-deductible, meaning that any money you contribute may reduce your taxable income, provided you meet income and eligibility requirements. In a traditional IRA, the contributions grow tax-deferred, which means you don't pay taxes on your gains until you start withdrawing funds, typically after age 59½.

For instance, if you're currently in a high tax bracket, a traditional IRA can help reduce your tax burden today, giving you more disposable income to invest or save. However, since you'll pay taxes when you withdraw the funds, this option may be more appealing if you expect to be in a lower tax bracket during retirement.

Roth IRA

A Roth IRA is similar to a traditional IRA but with a key difference in tax treatment. Unlike a traditional IRA, contributions to a Roth IRA are made with after-tax dollars, which means they're not deductible. However, the major advantage of a Roth IRA is that withdrawals in retirement are tax-free. This means any growth within a Roth IRA is untaxed when withdrawn, providing a potentially significant benefit, especially for younger investors with decades of compounding ahead of them.

The Roth IRA is often favored by those who expect to be in a higher tax bracket in retirement or by those who prioritize tax-free income later in life. Since contributions are made with after-tax dollars, you've already paid taxes on this income, so qualified withdrawals come out tax-free. Roth IRAs are also advantageous if you want flexibility, as they don't require minimum distributions in retirement.

401(k)

The 401(k) is a retirement plan sponsored by employers, which means you can only participate if your employer offers one. A 401(k) plan allows employees to contribute a portion of their income directly into the account, often with pre-tax dollars, similar to a traditional IRA. One major advantage of a 401(k) plan is that many employers offer a matching contribution, meaning they add a certain amount to your account based on what you contribute, up to a certain percentage. This employer match is essentially free money and can greatly increase your retirement savings.

A 401(k) can offer higher annual contribution limits than an IRA, making it especially attractive for those who want to save more aggressively for retirement. Additionally, some employers offer Roth 401(k) options, allowing you to make after-tax contributions to your 401(k) with the benefit of tax-free withdrawals in retirement.

Each of these accounts has unique benefits, and many investors use a combination of these to balance tax advantages now and in the future. Understanding these differences can help you create a retirement strategy that aligns with your personal goals and tax situation.

Tax Advantages: Lowering Taxable Income, Tax-Free Growth, and Choosing Based on Tax Bracket

Lowering Taxable Income

One of the primary benefits of traditional retirement accounts, such as a traditional IRA or 401(k), is the ability to lower your taxable income in the current year. For instance, if you contribute $5,000 to a traditional IRA and you're in the 22% tax bracket, your tax savings for that year would be around $1,100 (22%

of $5,000). By lowering your taxable income, you not only save on taxes but also retain more money in your pocket for saving, investing, or everyday expenses.

For high-income earners, lowering taxable income through retirement contributions is a valuable strategy. As income levels rise, the tax rate on that income increases, so any tax deduction can represent a significant benefit. For example, a 401(k) plan allows employees to contribute up to $22,500 annually (as of 2024), with that amount reducing their taxable income. Taking advantage of this deduction can make a substantial difference in a high-tax environment.

Tax-Free Growth with Roth Accounts

Roth IRAs and Roth 401(k)s do not provide tax deductions on contributions, but they offer another significant advantage: tax-free growth. Because you fund these accounts with after-tax dollars, your investments can grow tax-free, and withdrawals in retirement are also tax-free, provided you follow the rules for qualified withdrawals.

For younger investors or those in lower tax brackets, a Roth account can be an effective way to maximize long-term savings. The money grows without being subject to taxes, and since you've already paid taxes on the contributions, you can enjoy tax-free income in retirement. This is particularly beneficial if you expect to be in a higher tax bracket later, as you'll avoid paying those future taxes on your withdrawals.

Choosing Based on Tax Bracket

When selecting between a traditional and Roth account, it's crucial to consider your current and expected future tax bracket. If you're in a high tax bracket now and expect to be in a lower one in retirement, a traditional IRA or 401(k) may be more advantageous since you'll receive a tax break now and pay taxes later when your rate may be lower.

Conversely, if you're in a lower tax bracket now and expect your income to grow significantly over time, a Roth account may be the better option, as you pay taxes at today's lower rate and withdraw tax-free in retirement. Many investors use a mix of both account types to create tax diversification, ensuring they'll have both taxable and tax-free income sources in retirement.

Contribution Limits: Annual Caps, Strategies to Maximize Contributions, Avoiding Penalties

Annual Contribution Caps

Retirement accounts come with annual contribution limits, which cap how much you can save each year. For traditional and Roth IRAs, the limit is $6,500 in 2024 (with an additional $1,000 "catch-up" contribution allowed if you're 50 or older). 401(k) plans have higher contribution limits, allowing you to contribute up to $22,500, with an additional $7,500 catch-up contribution if you're over 50.

These contribution limits may seem restrictive, but maximizing them each year can add up significantly over time, especially with the compounding effect. For example, consistently maxing out a 401(k) could result in substantial retirement savings, especially if you start early and benefit from an employer match.

Strategies to Maximize Contributions

To make the most of retirement accounts, consider strategies to consistently reach or exceed your contribution limits. One effective strategy is to automate contributions, having a set amount deducted from your paycheck directly into your retirement accounts. This ensures you're contributing regularly without the temptation to spend elsewhere. Additionally, adjusting your contributions each year to account for increased limits or changes in income can help you stay on track.

If cash flow is tight, consider allocating any windfalls—such as tax refunds, bonuses, or gifts—toward your retirement accounts. These one-time contributions can give your retirement savings a boost without affecting your regular budget. For those with multiple income streams, such as a side business, you might consider establishing a SEP IRA or Solo 401(k), which offers higher contribution limits for self-employed individuals.

Avoiding Penalties

Retirement accounts come with rules around contributions and withdrawals, and violating these can lead to penalties. For example, withdrawing from a traditional IRA or 401(k) before age 59½ typically incurs a 10% early withdrawal penalty in addition to regular income taxes. This can significantly erode your savings, so it's essential to plan withdrawals carefully and, if needed, set up an emergency fund outside of retirement accounts.

Similarly, exceeding contribution limits can result in penalties. If you over-contribute to an IRA, you may face a 6% excise tax on the excess amount each year until it's corrected. To avoid this, keep a close eye on how much you're contributing, particularly if you're contributing to both a workplace retirement plan and an IRA, which can complicate the contribution limits for higher-income earners.

Planning, keeping track of contributions, and understanding these limits and rules can prevent costly mistakes, allowing you to keep more of your money growing for retirement.

Compounding Returns, Investment Choices, and Adjusting Risk Over Time

When it comes to securing a financially comfortable retirement, time and strategy are two of your best allies. The power of compounding, coupled with disciplined investment choices and a thoughtful approach to risk management, can enable your retirement accounts to grow exponentially. In this section, we'll explore why starting early is essential, the different types of investments you can make within retirement accounts, and how to adjust your risk profile as you get closer to retirement. By understanding these key elements, you'll be better prepared to make informed choices that support your long-term goals.

Compounding Returns: Importance of Early Contributions, Exponential Growth, and Consistency

Importance of Early Contributions

One of the most compelling reasons to start contributing to retirement accounts as early as possible is the power of compounding. Compounding is the process where your investment gains generate their own earnings over time, essentially creating a snowball effect. The longer your money stays invested, the more compounding works in your favor. Even if you can only contribute a small amount initially, starting early allows that money to grow significantly by the time you reach retirement age.

Consider the difference between someone who begins investing $5,000 per year at age 25 versus someone who starts at 35. Assuming an average return of 7%, the first investor will accumulate roughly $1 million by age 65, whereas the second investor, who contributed the same annual amount but started ten years later, will have around $500,000. That's half the amount, despite only a decade's difference in start time. This example underscores the value of starting as soon as possible, even if your initial contributions are modest.

Exponential Growth Over Time

The concept of exponential growth through compounding may seem abstract, but its effects become very tangible over time. Early in your investment journey, the growth might seem slow; however, the real power of compounding becomes evident in the later years as your earnings begin to compound on top of each other. As your account balance grows, even a 5% or 7% return represents a substantial dollar amount, creating more significant gains each year.

Take, for example, an initial balance of $10,000 growing at a 7% annual rate. In the first year, that balance grows by $700. But in the 20th year, the growth from compounding could add over $2,000 or more to your balance in just that single year, thanks to the increased account size and accumulated growth. This exponential growth can provide a powerful tailwind in your retirement savings plan, emphasizing the value of consistent investing.

Effects of Consistent Investing

Consistency is essential for long-term investment success. By investing regularly, even during market downturns, you benefit from dollar-cost averaging—purchasing shares at different prices over time, which can help you ride out market volatility and lower the average cost per share. Regular contributions, especially in tax-advantaged retirement accounts like a 401(k) or IRA, allow you to accumulate more assets over time without having to worry about market timing.

Moreover, consistent investing can become a steady habit that enhances your financial discipline. Setting up automatic contributions, whether through payroll deductions for a 401(k) or automatic transfers to an IRA, makes it easier to stay on track. Over time, your discipline in making these consistent contributions will likely yield substantial results as your balance grows, helping you reach retirement goals more efficiently.

Investment Choices: Options Within Retirement Accounts and Selecting Based on Retirement Horizon

Options Within Retirement Accounts

Retirement accounts often offer a variety of investment choices, including stocks, bonds, mutual funds, and exchange-traded funds (ETFs). Each of these investment types serves a different role in your portfolio and has varying levels of risk and return potential. For instance, stocks provide higher growth potential but also come with higher volatility. Bonds, on the other hand, are typically more stable but offer lower returns, which can serve as a safety net during volatile markets.

In many 401(k) plans, you can choose from a range of mutual funds or target-date funds. Target-date funds are designed to gradually reduce risk as you approach a target retirement year, making them a convenient choice for hands-off investors. In IRAs, especially self-directed ones, you have even more flexibility to pick individual stocks, ETFs, and bond funds, allowing you to create a diversified portfolio tailored to your specific goals and risk tolerance.

Selecting Based on Retirement Horizon

Your time horizon—the number of years until you need to start withdrawing from your retirement account—plays a major role in determining your investment choices. If you're decades away from retirement, you may want to focus on growth-oriented investments, like stocks or stock-based mutual funds, which have higher return potential despite their volatility. The reason is simple: with a longer timeline, you have the luxury of waiting out market downturns, giving your investments time to recover and grow.

As you approach retirement age, your investment strategy may shift toward preserving the wealth you've accumulated. Many investors start moving toward a more conservative mix of investments that includes bonds, which tend to provide steady income with less volatility. The goal is to protect your retirement savings from large fluctuations, ensuring you have the resources you'll need during retirement.

Balancing Growth and Stability

Finding the right balance between growth and stability is key to maximizing your retirement account's long-term potential. Early on, leaning heavily into stocks may make sense because the compounding effect can greatly enhance growth. Over time, however, balancing stocks with bonds or other low-risk investments can help you maintain stability and protect your assets from sharp declines. The mix you choose will ultimately depend on your unique financial situation, tolerance for risk, and retirement goals.

Adjusting Risk Over Time: Reducing Risk as Retirement Nears, Transitioning to Conservative Investments, and Maintaining Stability

Reducing Risk as Retirement Nears

As you get closer to retirement, the goal often shifts from growing your wealth to protecting it. Large market downturns can have a significant impact on your retirement savings, especially if they happen just before or during your retirement years, when you'll need to start drawing from your accounts. To minimize the risk of losing a substantial portion of your savings, consider gradually reducing your exposure to high-risk assets like stocks and increasing your holdings in safer, more stable assets.

This gradual reduction in risk is sometimes referred to as "glide path" investing, where you steadily decrease your allocation to equities and increase your allocation to fixed-income assets, such as bonds, as retirement approaches. By doing so, you create a more stable portfolio that is less likely to be affected by sudden market swings, helping ensure your funds last through retirement.

Transitioning to Conservative Investments

Transitioning to conservative investments doesn't necessarily mean eliminating all growth-oriented assets. Instead, it involves finding a balance that aligns with your need for income, your tolerance for risk, and your expected lifespan in retirement. Bonds and bond funds can provide predictable returns and preserve capital, while dividend-paying stocks can provide a steady income with some growth potential.

Many retirement planners also consider adding assets like real estate or income-generating funds that provide a combination of growth and income, offering stability with moderate appreciation potential. By maintaining a diverse array of conservative investments, you're not putting all your eggs in one basket, which can help protect your assets from market volatility.

Maintaining Stability and Adjusting to Your Life Stage

Maintaining stability in your retirement portfolio is a dynamic process that requires you to adjust your holdings based on your current life stage and needs. During early and middle phases of retirement, you might still keep a small percentage of your portfolio in equities to benefit from potential growth and hedge against inflation. However, as you progress further into retirement, you may reduce this exposure further, relying more heavily on fixed-income investments to provide a stable income stream.

Regularly reviewing and rebalancing your portfolio is essential for maintaining this stability. It's common to review your asset allocation annually or semi-annually, making adjustments as needed to ensure your portfolio aligns with your changing risk tolerance and financial needs. By proactively managing your risk, you can create a retirement portfolio that supports your goals while providing peace of mind.

Required Minimum Distributions, Withdrawal Strategies, and Tax-Efficient Withdrawals

As you approach retirement, the way you handle withdrawals from your retirement accounts becomes as crucial as how you invest in them. Planning withdrawals requires a deep understanding of rules such as Required Minimum Distributions (RMDs), effective withdrawal strategies to maintain your account balance, and tax-efficient tactics to minimize the impact on your income. Properly managing these elements can make the difference between a comfortable retirement and one with financial stress. Let's explore these aspects in detail so you can maximize the value of your retirement savings while ensuring your funds last as long as you need them.

Required Minimum Distributions (RMDs): When They Apply, Planning for Withdrawals, and Tax Implications

When RMDs Apply

RMDs are mandated withdrawals that begin at a certain age for certain types of retirement accounts, including Traditional IRAs, SEP IRAs, SIMPLE IRAs, and most 401(k) plans. Under current U.S. laws, RMDs generally start at age 73, although the starting age could change in the future. RMDs exist because retirement accounts like traditional IRAs and 401(k)s are tax-deferred, meaning you didn't pay taxes on the money you contributed or on its growth. The government requires these distributions so it can begin collecting taxes on your retirement funds.

Knowing when RMDs apply is essential, as missing an RMD or taking less than the required amount can lead to substantial penalties. The IRS currently imposes a 25% excise tax on the amount not withdrawn following RMD rules, and this penalty can be reduced to 10% if corrected on time. Staying informed about RMD requirements ensures you avoid these penalties, enabling you to retain more of your retirement funds.

Planning for Withdrawals

Planning for RMDs involves more than just knowing when they start; it requires a strategic approach to ensure that withdrawals align with your financial goals and tax situation. RMDs are calculated each year based on your account balance and life expectancy. Since the amount you're required to withdraw can vary annually, it's wise to include RMDs in your retirement income planning, forecasting future withdrawal amounts to anticipate how they'll impact your cash flow.

For many retirees, the RMD amount aligns with or exceeds their annual living expenses, meaning they may need to adjust other income sources to avoid over-accumulating funds in taxable accounts. If you don't need to spend the RMD amount, consider transferring it to a non-retirement investment account, where you can continue growing your assets without being subject to the RMD rules. Planning around RMDs can allow you to maintain control over your finances while staying compliant with tax regulations.

Tax Implications of RMDs

Understanding the tax implications of RMDs is essential because these withdrawals are treated as ordinary income and can potentially push you into a higher tax bracket. If your RMDs are substantial, the increase in taxable income could have a domino effect, impacting not only your federal income tax rate but also Medicare premiums and other tax-related areas. For example, if your adjusted gross income (AGI) rises above certain thresholds, you might be subject to Medicare surcharges or increased taxes on Social Security benefits.

To minimize tax impact, some retirees look into Roth conversions before RMDs begin. Converting a portion of your traditional IRA to a Roth IRA can reduce the balance of your traditional accounts, ultimately lowering your future RMDs. Although Roth conversions generate taxable income at the time of conversion, Roth accounts do not have RMD requirements, and qualified withdrawals from Roth IRAs are tax-free. Proper planning around RMDs can help you manage tax liabilities and preserve more of your retirement income.

Withdrawal Strategies: Managing Withdrawals, Creating Cash Flow, and Sustaining Your Account Balance

Managing Withdrawals to Avoid Penalties

One of the key strategies for retirement is to carefully manage withdrawals in a way that prevents penalties and maximizes income. Most retirement accounts penalize early withdrawals before age 59½, with a 10% penalty in addition to income taxes on the amount withdrawn. While RMDs ensure that you must take withdrawals starting at age 73, being aware of the early withdrawal penalties can prevent costly mistakes if you're accessing funds before retirement age.

If you need to tap into retirement funds early, consider using exceptions to avoid penalties. For example, if you're leaving your job at age 55 or older, you can access funds from your 401(k) without incurring early withdrawal penalties, though this exception doesn't apply to IRAs. By structuring withdrawals to avoid penalties, you'll preserve more of your funds for later years when you may need them most.

Converting Withdrawals into Cash Flow

For many retirees, managing withdrawals effectively means creating a steady cash flow that supports their lifestyle while keeping enough funds invested for growth. A sustainable withdrawal rate—commonly around 4% annually—has traditionally been considered a guideline for withdrawing from retirement accounts. This rate aims to balance the need for income with the need to preserve capital, providing income while leaving funds for future growth.

When planning your cash flow, it's wise to consider withdrawing from taxable accounts first, followed by tax-deferred accounts, and finally tax-free accounts (like Roth IRAs). This order helps manage your tax liability each year, giving you the flexibility to withdraw what you need without incurring unnecessary taxes. Converting your withdrawals into reliable cash flow requires planning but can lead to a stable and sustainable income throughout your retirement.

Sustaining Your Account Balance

One of the biggest concerns retirees face is the risk of outliving their savings. To avoid this, consider using strategies that help maintain your account balance over time. The 4% rule provides a starting point, but it's not a one-size-fits-all answer. During market downturns, you might reduce withdrawals temporarily, while in strong market years, you might allow yourself more flexibility.

In addition to maintaining a moderate withdrawal rate, ensuring that you rebalance your portfolio periodically can help sustain your account. By rebalancing, you adjust your asset mix to match your risk tolerance and financial needs, which helps protect your account balance against large market swings. Sustaining your balance takes planning and discipline, but it can provide peace of mind and financial stability in retirement.

Tax-Efficient Withdrawals: Minimizing Taxes, Roth vs. Traditional IRA Withdrawals, and Sequencing Withdrawals

Minimizing Tax Impact

Withdrawing retirement funds in a tax-efficient manner can have a major impact on your overall retirement income. By minimizing the taxes on your withdrawals, you effectively increase the amount of money available for your use. One strategy to consider is tax-loss harvesting, where you sell investments at a loss in taxable accounts to offset gains, potentially reducing your taxable income. Another approach is to time your withdrawals in low-income years, which may keep you in a lower tax bracket.

Additionally, retirees who fall within a low tax bracket may benefit from converting portions of traditional IRA funds to Roth IRAs in these low-income years. Although conversions are taxable events, completing them at a low tax rate allows your Roth account to grow tax-free, which can reduce your taxable income in future years. Small, strategic conversions over time can provide tax efficiency while securing more tax-free retirement income.

Roth vs. Traditional IRA Withdrawals

When choosing between Roth and traditional IRA withdrawals, understanding the tax implications can help you make the most of your retirement income. Traditional IRAs offer tax-deductible contributions, but all withdrawals are taxed as ordinary income. In contrast, Roth IRAs provide no upfront tax break, but qualified withdrawals are tax-free, which can provide flexibility in managing taxable income in retirement.

For retirees aiming to minimize tax impact, it may be beneficial to withdraw from traditional IRAs during lower-income years and from Roth IRAs when higher tax brackets would apply. This flexibility in choosing between tax-deferred and tax-free income sources enables you to manage your tax exposure effectively. By strategically using both types of accounts, you can maximize tax savings while sustaining your retirement lifestyle.

Sequencing Withdrawals to Save on Taxes

The order in which you withdraw from various accounts can significantly influence your tax liability. Tax-efficient sequencing typically follows the order of using taxable accounts first, then tax-deferred accounts (like traditional IRAs and 401(k)s), and finally tax-free accounts, such as Roth IRAs. This sequence allows taxable accounts to be depleted first, avoiding taxes on gains as early as possible. It also lets tax-deferred accounts grow longer, which can be beneficial for future income.

During market downturns or years with substantial taxable gains, tapping into Roth accounts provides tax-free income, helping you avoid unnecessary taxes. By adhering to a tax-efficient withdrawal sequence, you may reduce your lifetime tax bill, leaving more of your money to grow and support your retirement needs. In addition, a thoughtful sequence can help manage your marginal tax rate, further protecting your income.

Chapter 6: Real Estate Investing

Real estate can be a powerful addition to any investment portfolio, providing diversification, the potential for income, and tangible assets that often appreciate over time. The world of real estate investing is broad, offering options that range from owning physical property to participating in real estate markets through investments like Real Estate Investment Trusts (REITs) and real estate crowdfunding platforms. Each of these options comes with unique benefits and considerations, allowing investors to choose what aligns best with their goals, risk tolerance, and financial resources.

Buying Property: Residential vs. Commercial, Benefits of Rental Properties, and Income Potential

Residential vs. Commercial Properties

Investing in real estate can mean purchasing either residential or commercial properties, each with distinct characteristics and benefits. Residential real estate generally refers to properties intended for individuals or families to live in, like single-family homes, duplexes, apartments, and condominiums. Residential properties tend to be more accessible for beginners, as they often have lower initial costs and financing options that are more favorable for first-time investors. Residential real estate also often benefits from consistent demand, as people always need housing, making it an attractive choice for those seeking a relatively stable investment.

Commercial properties, on the other hand, include office buildings, retail spaces, warehouses, and multi-unit complexes. While commercial real estate requires a larger upfront investment and more complex management, it can offer higher potential returns. Commercial leases tend to be longer and can bring in steady cash flow from businesses, reducing the vacancy risk compared to residential properties. However, the commercial sector can be more sensitive to economic changes, as businesses may be more likely to close or move during economic downturns, potentially impacting rental income. Investors with a higher risk tolerance and financial flexibility may find the potential gains from commercial properties worth exploring.

Benefits of Owning Rental Properties

Owning rental property can be an effective way to generate passive income, offering both monthly cash flow from rent and potential long-term appreciation of the property's value. Rental income can supplement other income streams and contribute significantly to building wealth over time. Additionally, property values have historically appreciated, meaning that, over the long term, the value of your investment can increase, especially in areas experiencing growth or revitalization.

Investing in rental properties also allows you to leverage your capital. By using mortgage financing, you can control an asset worth significantly more than your initial investment, amplifying your returns. For example, with a 20% down payment on a $200,000 property, you control the full value of the property while investing just $40,000 upfront. As you pay down the mortgage, your equity in the property increases, and you can eventually own it outright. However, managing a rental property does require time, commitment, and potentially handling tenant-related issues, which can add to the complexity.

Income Potential

Real estate's income potential makes it particularly appealing. Rental properties provide a steady stream of income, and when managed well, this cash flow can exceed the property's expenses, leaving you with profit each month. The income potential for real estate investments is often driven by location, property condition, and market demand. In high-demand areas with limited housing supply, rental rates can increase, which can improve cash flow.

Moreover, some investors choose to renovate properties to increase their value and command higher rents, known as "value-add" investing. For instance, updating kitchens or bathrooms in a residential rental can attract higher-paying tenants, while upgrading commercial properties can help you lease space to more reputable businesses at premium rates. The income generated by real estate can offer financial stability, as it is relatively predictable, particularly if you have reliable tenants. For retirees or those seeking financial independence, rental income can provide a solid foundation of cash flow that supports lifestyle expenses.

Real Estate Investment Trusts (REITs): How They Work, Benefits, and Types to Consider

How REITs Work

Real Estate Investment Trusts (REITs) are companies that own, operate, or finance income-producing real estate. They pool capital from multiple investors to buy and manage real estate assets, allowing individuals to invest in large-scale properties without directly buying or managing real estate. REITs are traded on major stock exchanges like stocks, making them highly liquid and accessible to anyone with a brokerage account.

The structure of REITs is unique: they are required by law to distribute at least 90% of their taxable income to shareholders in the form of dividends. This legal structure provides regular income to investors and makes REITs an attractive choice for those seeking consistent cash flow from real estate without the responsibilities of property management. By investing in REITs, investors can participate in the real estate market and gain exposure to different property types without the commitment and capital required for direct ownership.

Benefits of REITs

One of the primary benefits of REITs is their accessibility. Unlike buying property, which can require significant initial investment, REITs can be purchased in small amounts, making them an ideal option for beginner investors or those looking to diversify without high upfront costs. REITs also offer diversification within real estate, as many REITs own a variety of properties across sectors, reducing risk exposure to any single asset type.

Additionally, the dividend income generated by REITs can provide a steady source of income, making them attractive for income-focused investors, such as retirees. Because REITs trade on stock exchanges, they can be bought or sold at any time during market hours, providing liquidity that is generally not available with direct real estate investments. The combination of steady income and liquidity makes REITs a flexible and attractive option for those interested in real estate.

Types of REITs to Consider

REITs come in several types, each focused on different segments of the real estate market. Equity REITs own and manage properties, generating income through leasing and property appreciation. Mortgage REITs (mREITs), on the other hand, focus on financing real estate by investing in mortgages and mortgage-backed securities. Hybrid REITs combine elements of both, holding properties and investing in mortgages.

Specialty REITs focus on niche markets, such as healthcare facilities, data centers, and storage spaces, which can offer exposure to high-demand sectors. Publicly traded REITs are most common, but private REITs and public non-traded REITs are also available, though they come with liquidity restrictions. Each type of REIT has unique risk and return profiles, allowing investors to choose one that aligns with their risk tolerance and investment objectives.

Real Estate Crowdfunding: Basics, Benefits, and Risks

Basics of Crowdfunding

Real estate crowdfunding has emerged as a modern way to invest in real estate through online platforms, enabling individuals to invest in properties by pooling funds with other investors. Crowdfunding platforms offer various types of real estate investments, from residential developments to commercial projects, and often allow investors to choose specific projects to back. This option is ideal for individuals who may not have the capital or desire to purchase property outright but still want exposure to real estate.

Crowdfunding platforms typically work by allowing investors to buy into individual deals or funds, with minimum investments starting as low as a few hundred dollars. Many platforms conduct due diligence on projects before listing them, though investors should always perform their research. Crowdfunding offers accessibility and the ability to invest in specific real estate assets, making it a viable option for smaller investors seeking targeted exposure to real estate.

Benefits of Real Estate Crowdfunding

One of the primary benefits of real estate crowdfunding is accessibility. With lower minimum investments, individuals can participate in high-quality real estate projects that would otherwise be out of reach. Crowdfunding platforms also provide a high level of transparency, giving investors access to detailed information about each project, such as financial projections, timelines, and market analyses, allowing for informed decision-making.

Crowdfunding can also offer portfolio diversification, as it allows investors to spread their capital across multiple projects or property types, rather than tying up a large sum in a single property.

Furthermore, many real estate crowdfunding investments are structured to provide returns through a combination of income distributions and appreciation, allowing investors to benefit from cash flow while holding an asset that may appreciate over time.

Risks of Crowdfunding

While crowdfunding presents exciting opportunities, it's not without risks. Unlike highly liquid REITs, real estate crowdfunding investments are generally illiquid, meaning your money is tied up for the duration of the project, which could be several years. Additionally, while many platforms vet projects, real estate ventures are inherently risky and dependent on market conditions, developer experience, and project execution.

Crowdfunding also typically involves high fees, which can cut into returns. Investors may face management fees, platform fees, and profit-sharing with developers. It's essential to thoroughly understand the fees, timelines, and risk factors associated with any investment. Carefully selecting crowdfunding projects and platforms can mitigate some risks, but investors should approach real estate crowdfunding with realistic expectations and a willingness to accept potential volatility.

Evaluating Real Estate Investments

The success of real estate investments often hinges on thorough evaluation. Unlike more traditional assets like stocks and bonds, real estate requires investors to consider physical and market factors, which can significantly impact returns and long-term value. From understanding the critical role of location to calculating cash flow and mastering leverage, this section focuses on evaluating real estate investments to make informed and strategic decisions.

Location Importance: Key Factors in Property Location, Market Trends, and Aligning Location with Goals

In real estate, the phrase "location, location, location" is more than a saying—it's a guiding principle. The location of a property can heavily influence its value, demand, and overall potential for appreciation. Investors must carefully analyze location factors to align their real estate purchases with their investment objectives, whether that means stable rental income, long-term value growth, or a mix of both.

Key Factors in Property Location

When evaluating a property's location, consider several essential factors that can influence both short-term rental demand and long-term value. Proximity to schools, parks, public transportation, and shopping centers typically attracts tenants, making properties in such areas more likely to experience consistent demand. For instance, a property close to a major university might yield high demand from students and faculty, while one near downtown areas or business districts may appeal to working professionals.

Safety and neighborhood reputation also play a role. Crime rates, the quality of local amenities, and the appearance of the neighborhood can significantly impact both rental demand and resale value. Areas with a reputation for being safe and having a strong community often command higher rents and experience more stable occupancy rates. Additionally, the infrastructure and growth potential of the neighborhood matter; investing in an area with planned development projects, like new highways, shopping centers, or corporate campuses, can lead to higher appreciation and rental demand as the neighborhood grows.

Market Trends

Understanding local and national real estate trends is essential for evaluating the potential success of a property investment. For example, if a city is experiencing rapid population growth and job creation, properties within that city may appreciate faster than properties in stagnant or declining areas. Studying housing demand in the area, as well as local market conditions, can help investors avoid overpaying during market peaks or missing out on high-potential areas.

Market trends also involve analyzing rental trends, vacancy rates, and historical appreciation. A property in a neighborhood with a low vacancy rate indicates high demand, making it easier to secure tenants. Similarly, high rental growth rates can signal a good investment environment, as increased rents lead to higher returns on rental properties. By keeping an eye on both macro (national) and micro (local) trends, investors can gain insights into the potential performance of a property over time.

Aligning Location with Goals

Each location will offer different investment potential, depending on an investor's goals. For those focused on rental income, a property in a highly populated urban area with a steady demand for rentals might be ideal. On the other hand, investors looking for appreciation might target up-and-coming neighborhoods where property values are likely to increase in the future.

For example, if your primary goal is cash flow, you might prioritize areas with strong rental demand and affordable property prices, such as suburban neighborhoods with good schools and convenient commuting options. For appreciation-focused investors, targeting areas undergoing revitalization, where property values have room to grow, can offer better returns on capital growth. Location choice, therefore, depends on understanding how your goals align with the specific attributes of the area.

Calculating Cash Flow: Rental Income vs. Expenses, Estimating Potential ROI, and Importance of Positive Cash Flow

Evaluating the potential for cash flow is a fundamental part of assessing any rental property. Cash flow is the amount of money left after accounting for rental income minus expenses, and it's a vital metric to determine whether a property will be a profitable investment. By calculating cash flow accurately, investors can understand the financial health of a property and make decisions that support consistent, positive returns.

Rental Income vs. Expenses

To determine the potential cash flow from a rental property, begin by estimating the rental income. This can involve researching comparable rentals in the area to get a realistic view of what tenants are willing to pay. For example, if nearby properties with similar features rent for $1,500 per month, that's a good indicator of potential rental income.

On the expenses side, include mortgage payments, property taxes, insurance, maintenance, and any management fees if you're hiring a property manager. Other expenses to account for include vacancy rates (the cost of unoccupied periods), repair costs, and utilities if they're covered by the landlord. It's common to underestimate these expenses, so adding a buffer can provide a more accurate cash flow picture.

Estimating Potential ROI

Beyond calculating monthly cash flow, evaluating a property's return on investment (ROI) offers insights into its profitability over time. ROI takes the net profit generated by the property and compares it to the initial investment, typically expressed as a percentage. Calculating ROI for rental properties includes factoring in annual cash flow, property appreciation, and tax benefits.

For instance, if you purchase a property for $200,000 and invest an additional $20,000 in renovations, your total investment is $220,000. If the property generates a net annual income of $15,000 and appreciates by 3% ($6,600) each year, your ROI would combine these returns to give a fuller picture of potential profitability. Comparing the ROI of different properties can help in identifying the most financially sound investments and understanding their potential for future growth.

Importance of Positive Cash Flow

Positive cash flow means that after all expenses are paid, the property generates profit. Achieving positive cash flow is essential, especially for investors looking to build a sustainable real estate portfolio.

Positive cash flow provides income stability and financial flexibility, allowing investors to reinvest in other properties or cover unexpected costs without stress.

Real estate investments with negative cash flow can become a financial burden if they require constant capital injections. By focusing on properties that generate positive cash flow from the outset, investors can build a portfolio that gradually increases wealth and reduces risk. Positive cash flow also provides a cushion against market downturns, allowing investors to maintain their investments even during challenging times.

Understanding Leverage: Mortgage Basics, Using Leverage to Maximize Returns, and Risks of Over-Leveraging

Leverage is one of real estate's most attractive aspects, allowing investors to control larger assets with a smaller initial investment through the use of mortgages. Understanding leverage is crucial for maximizing returns and minimizing risks. When used wisely, leverage can amplify returns, but over-leveraging can also lead to increased risks, especially in volatile markets.

Mortgage Basics

A mortgage is a loan used to purchase real estate, where the property itself serves as collateral. Mortgages allow investors to buy properties without paying the full price upfront, providing the opportunity to invest in larger or multiple properties than would be possible with cash alone. Mortgages typically come with fixed or variable interest rates, and investors make monthly payments over a predetermined term.

For example, with a 20% down payment on a $200,000 property, you control a $200,000 asset by investing only $40,000. The remaining $160,000 is borrowed through a mortgage. Each month, a portion of the rental income generated by the property goes toward paying down the mortgage. By reducing the debt over time, the investor gradually builds equity in the property, and ideally, the property appreciates.

Using Leverage to Maximize Returns

Leverage can enhance an investor's returns by amplifying the potential gains from a property's appreciation. For instance, if a leveraged property appreciates by 10% in a year, the return on the investor's initial down payment could be much higher than 10%, depending on the leverage amount. This potential to control a valuable asset with a smaller initial investment is one of the reasons real estate can produce substantial returns over time.

Leverage allows investors to grow their portfolios by freeing up capital that can be allocated toward additional properties. By spreading investments across multiple properties, investors diversify their portfolios, reducing the impact of a single property's underperformance. However, it's essential to carefully evaluate each property's cash flow to ensure it can cover mortgage payments and other expenses, especially if interest rates fluctuate or rental income dips.

Risks of Over-Leveraging

While leverage can enhance returns, over-leveraging carries substantial risks. A highly leveraged property can quickly become a liability if rental income falls short of mortgage payments or if property values decline. In such cases, the investor may struggle to meet mortgage obligations, leading to potential foreclosure or a need to sell at a loss.

To avoid the dangers of over-leveraging, it's essential to maintain a balance between debt and equity. Many experienced investors use the "50% rule," where they avoid leveraging more than 50% of their portfolio's total value. This provides a cushion in the event of market downturns or unexpected vacancies. By leveraging carefully and conservatively, investors can take advantage of leverage's benefits without overexposing themselves to financial risk.

Managing Real Estate Investments

Investing in real estate is just the beginning; successful management is the key to ensuring your properties remain profitable and valuable. Effective management involves not only overseeing the property itself but also handling tenant relationships, budgeting for maintenance, and planning the right exit strategy when it's time to sell. In this section, we'll explore essential aspects of managing real estate investments, from property management and maintenance to developing exit strategies that help maximize your investment's potential.

Property Management: Self-Management vs. Hiring Managers, Managing Tenants, and Responsibilities as a Landlord

Once a property is acquired, the decision of whether to self-manage or hire a property management company is one of the first major considerations. The responsibilities of a landlord extend beyond collecting rent; they include tenant management, property maintenance, legal compliance, and more. Balancing these duties is crucial to maintaining a profitable and hassle-free investment.

Self-Management vs. Hiring Property Managers
Managing a property yourself can save money on fees, but it also requires time, effort, and a willingness to take on a range of duties. Self-managing landlords are responsible for finding tenants, setting rent rates, collecting rent, handling repairs, and addressing tenant issues. For investors who live near their properties and have the time to dedicate to management, self-managing can be a cost-effective way

to increase returns. For example, if you have a single rental property nearby, the time investment may be manageable, and the added monthly income from not paying a management fee can boost profitability.

However, as portfolios grow, self-management can become overwhelming. Property managers handle tenant screenings, rental collections, legal compliance, and property maintenance, among other duties. Hiring a management company is often ideal for those who own multiple properties or who live far from their rental properties. Although they typically charge a monthly fee (around 8-12% of the rental income), property managers allow investors to have a more hands-off approach. For many, the peace of mind and efficiency that a professional manager provides is worth the cost, especially for busy investors or those new to rental properties.

Managing Tenants

Tenant management is one of the most critical aspects of real estate investing. Happy tenants are more likely to renew leases, take care of the property, and pay rent on time. Screening prospective tenants carefully can prevent issues down the line. This includes checking references, employment, and rental history to ensure tenants can meet their obligations.

Once tenants move in, clear communication is key to maintaining a positive relationship. Make sure they understand the lease terms, including rent due dates, property rules, and maintenance procedures. For example, some landlords set up an online portal where tenants can pay rent, submit maintenance requests, and receive announcements. Providing a convenient and professional system helps build trust and reduces misunderstandings, ensuring a smoother experience for both parties.

Responsibilities as a Landlord

Being a landlord carries various legal and ethical responsibilities. Laws vary by location, but landlords are generally required to provide safe, habitable living conditions, handle repairs promptly, and respect tenants' privacy rights. In addition to legal compliance, many landlords establish policies on routine maintenance inspections and tenant communication to ensure the property remains in good condition and that any issues are addressed promptly.

Moreover, understanding local tenant rights and regulations is essential to avoiding legal disputes. For instance, landlords must follow specific procedures for issuing notices, collecting late fees, and returning security deposits. Violating tenant rights, even unintentionally, can lead to costly penalties and lawsuits. By staying informed and professional, landlords can foster a positive, lawful rental experience that protects their investments and reputation.

Maintenance and Repairs: Budgeting for Repairs, Ensuring Property Value, and Tax Implications of Maintenance

Keeping a property well-maintained is essential for preserving its value and ensuring tenant satisfaction. Maintenance can be unpredictable, and investors must budget accordingly to handle both routine upkeep and unexpected repairs. From minor repairs to significant renovations, managing maintenance wisely can directly impact profitability and the property's long-term worth.

Budgeting for Repairs

Every rental property requires ongoing maintenance, and budgeting for these expenses is essential for avoiding financial strain. Many investors follow the "1% rule," which suggests setting aside 1% of the property's value each year for maintenance costs. For example, if your property is worth $200,000, aim to budget $2,000 annually for repairs. However, this rule is a rough guideline, and the actual amount needed may vary based on the property's age, condition, and location.

In addition to annual budgeting, it's wise to create an emergency fund specifically for larger repairs. Major expenses, like replacing a roof or HVAC system, can be costly, and having funds set aside helps ensure these repairs can be handled without disrupting cash flow. Proactively saving for significant repairs allows investors to keep the property in good shape without facing financial surprises.

Ensuring Property Value

Regular maintenance not only keeps tenants satisfied but also preserves the property's value. Routine inspections help landlords catch small issues before they escalate into costly repairs. For example, addressing a minor plumbing leak promptly can prevent extensive water damage, which would be far more expensive to repair. Similarly, performing preventative maintenance on heating and cooling systems can extend their lifespan, reducing the likelihood of sudden, high-cost replacements.

Enhancing a property's curb appeal and functionality through periodic upgrades also adds value. Simple improvements, such as fresh paint, landscaping, or updating fixtures, can attract quality tenants and justify higher rental rates. By investing in the property's upkeep and appearance, landlords can increase demand and improve the property's long-term value.

Tax Implications of Maintenance

One advantage of property maintenance is the potential tax benefits. Many maintenance and repair expenses are deductible, reducing the taxable income generated by the rental property. However, it's essential to understand the distinction between repairs and improvements, as these categories have different tax treatments.

Repairs, like fixing a leaky faucet or replacing a broken window, are generally tax-deductible in the year they occur. In contrast, improvements—like installing a new HVAC system or remodeling a kitchen—are typically capitalized and depreciated over time. Properly categorizing maintenance expenses can maximize tax benefits, making it worthwhile to consult a tax professional for guidance. Keeping accurate records of all repair and maintenance expenses is crucial for claiming deductions and ensuring compliance with tax regulations.

Exit Strategies: Selling Property, Timing for Maximum Profit, and Understanding Market Conditions

Real estate investors must also plan for the end of an investment. Whether an investor intends to hold a property indefinitely or sell it to capitalize on appreciation, having a clear exit strategy ensures that decisions align with financial goals. Understanding when and how to sell a property can maximize profits and support long-term wealth-building goals.

Selling Property

Selling a property is a significant decision, and timing the sale can impact the returns realized on the investment. Many investors choose to sell properties after a period of appreciation or when they've achieved their investment objectives. For example, if an investor purchased a property intending to hold it for 10 years and benefit from appreciation, selling once that goal is met may be optimal.

However, investors should also consider tax implications when selling. Capital gains taxes apply to the profit made on a property's sale, so it's essential to calculate potential tax liabilities. Some investors use a 1031 exchange—a tax-deferral strategy that allows them to reinvest the proceeds into a new property without paying capital gains taxes immediately. This approach can help investors continue growing their portfolios without tax burdens.

Timing for Maximum Profit

Market timing plays a crucial role in maximizing returns from a property sale. While predicting the exact peaks and troughs of the real estate market can be challenging, investors can monitor local and national trends to make informed timing decisions. Selling during a seller's market—when demand is high, and inventory is low—often allows investors to command higher prices and sell quickly.

Property value can also be influenced by factors like local development, interest rates, and economic conditions. For example, selling in a rapidly developing neighborhood or during a period of low interest rates may attract more buyers, driving up property prices. Conversely, selling during an economic downturn or in a neighborhood experiencing decline may result in lower offers. By understanding market cycles and timing sales strategically, investors can maximize their returns.

Understanding Market Conditions

Investors should stay informed about market conditions to gauge the ideal time to buy or sell. Real estate markets are affected by economic trends, interest rates, population growth, and regional developments, all of which can influence property values. For instance, if a city is experiencing an influx of new businesses and residents, property values may rise as demand for housing increases.

Monitoring indicators like vacancy rates, rent growth, and property appreciation trends in the area provides insight into the market's health. Tools such as Comparative Market Analysis (CMA) reports and local real estate data help investors assess current market values. Analyzing these conditions helps investors choose when to hold, sell, or even expand their portfolios based on market potential and economic indicators.

Chapter 7: Risk Management and Insurance

Investing is about achieving growth, but it also involves various risks. To navigate these effectively, a well-rounded approach to assessing risks is essential. This involves identifying potential investment risks, evaluating your personal risk tolerance, and understanding how your investment timeframe aligns with risk. In this section, we'll explore strategies for assessing and managing investment risks to help you build a resilient, growth-oriented portfolio.

Identifying Investment Risks: Market, Credit, and Inflation Risks; Knowing Your Tolerance; Reducing Exposure

Every investment carries an inherent level of risk, but understanding the types of risks can help you make informed decisions and create a balanced investment strategy. By learning to recognize these risks, you can find ways to mitigate them, aligning your investments with your goals and financial comfort level.

Market Risk

Market risk, or the risk of losing money due to fluctuations in the financial markets, is one of the most common risks investors face. This type of risk is particularly pronounced in investments that are heavily influenced by market trends, such as stocks and mutual funds. For example, during an economic downturn, stock prices may drop across the board, affecting the value of your portfolio. However, understanding that market risk is part of a long-term investment journey can help you manage it more effectively. One way to mitigate market risk is through diversification—spreading your investments across different sectors or asset types can help reduce the impact of a downturn in any single area.

Credit Risk

Credit risk applies mainly to bonds and other debt instruments. It's the risk that the issuer of the bond (such as a corporation or government entity) may default on its payments, affecting your returns. Credit risk can be managed by choosing high-quality bonds, such as government or highly-rated corporate bonds, as well as by diversifying your fixed-income investments. For example, investing in a mix of government bonds and AAA-rated corporate bonds reduces the potential impact of any one issuer's default. Additionally, bond ratings from agencies like Moody's or Standard & Poor's provide insights into the creditworthiness of bond issuers, helping investors make more secure choices.

Inflation Risk

Inflation risk is the danger that the rising cost of goods and services will erode the purchasing power of your money over time. This risk is particularly relevant to conservative investments like bonds or savings accounts, which may not keep pace with inflation. While bonds offer steady, predictable returns, they may fail to protect your investment's real value if inflation rates are high. To counter inflation risk, some investors allocate a portion of their portfolio to assets that historically outpace inflation, such as stocks or real estate. Balancing low-risk bonds with growth-oriented stocks or inflation-protected securities can help preserve your purchasing power in the long run.

Understanding these risks helps you make more calculated investment choices. Acknowledging that all investments come with some level of risk, knowing your tolerance, and implementing measures like diversification, can make navigating these risks more manageable.

Evaluating Risk Tolerance: How to Measure Tolerance, Adjusting Investments, Understanding Emotional Impact

Risk tolerance is your ability and willingness to endure investment losses in pursuit of greater returns. Evaluating your risk tolerance is essential for selecting the types of investments that match your comfort level and financial goals. Knowing where you stand on the risk spectrum can help you create a portfolio that aligns with both your personal and financial objectives.

How to Measure Tolerance

Measuring your risk tolerance often involves assessing your financial goals, time horizon, and emotional comfort with potential losses. Some investors find it helpful to use online risk tolerance questionnaires offered by brokerages or financial advisors. These questionnaires typically ask about your reactions to market downturns, your investment objectives, and your experience with investing. Answering these questions can reveal whether you're naturally conservative, aggressive, or somewhere in between in your investment approach. Additionally, reviewing your current investments and how you feel about their performance can provide insights into your true comfort level with risk.

Adjusting Investments to Match Tolerance

Once you've assessed your risk tolerance, you can adjust your portfolio to reflect it. For example, if you have a high tolerance for risk, you might allocate a larger portion of your investments to stocks, which can offer higher returns but come with greater volatility. Conversely, if you're more conservative, you might prefer bonds or dividend-paying stocks, which provide more stability but with potentially lower growth. It's also important to remember that your risk tolerance can change over time based on life circumstances, financial goals, and market experience. Regularly reassessing your tolerance and adjusting your portfolio can help you stay aligned with your evolving comfort level.

Understanding the Emotional Impact of Risk

Investment losses can be emotionally challenging, especially if they occur in a volatile market. Some investors are prone to panic selling or making impulsive decisions when markets fluctuate, which can lead to unnecessary losses. Recognizing that emotional reactions are part of investing can help you prepare for them. For example, setting clear goals and having a long-term perspective can make it easier to weather market downturns without feeling the urge to make hasty decisions. Staying informed and having a realistic understanding of market cycles can also reinforce the importance of maintaining a steady investment approach, even during turbulent times.

Evaluating your risk tolerance and understanding its impact on your investment behavior can help you build a portfolio that's not only financially viable but also emotionally manageable. This balance is key to sustaining your commitment to your investment strategy over the long term.

Time Horizon and Risk: Aligning Investments with Timeframes, Adjusting Strategy Over Time, Managing Expectations

Your investment time horizon—the period you plan to hold investments before needing to access the funds—plays a significant role in determining the appropriate level of risk for your portfolio. Matching your investment choices with your time horizon helps ensure you're taking a suitable amount of risk, maximizing growth potential while managing exposure to volatility.

Aligning Investments with Timeframes

The longer your time horizon, the more risk you can typically afford to take. For instance, younger investors saving for retirement 30 years in the future may invest heavily in stocks, which offer higher growth potential but also come with more volatility. In contrast, someone nearing retirement might prioritize stability and income-generating investments, such as bonds or dividend-paying stocks, to protect their assets. By aligning your investments with your time horizon, you increase the likelihood of achieving your financial goals while minimizing the chances of having to sell at a loss due to market fluctuations.

Adjusting Strategy Over Time

As your time horizon shortens, it's wise to gradually reduce the level of risk in your portfolio. This strategy, often called a "glide path," involves shifting from high-growth assets like stocks to more conservative investments, such as bonds or money market funds. For example, an investor with 20 years to retirement might hold a portfolio that's 80% stocks and 20% bonds. However, as they approach retirement, they may adjust to a 60/40 or even 50/50 allocation, depending on their income needs and risk tolerance. Rebalancing periodically to align with your current life stage can provide greater financial security as you near important goals, like funding retirement or a child's education.

Managing Expectations

Setting realistic expectations for investment returns based on your time horizon is essential for long-term satisfaction with your portfolio. Understanding that short-term investments may not deliver significant growth—and that long-term investments require patience and resilience—helps prevent frustration. For instance, if you're investing in a stock market index fund with a 20-year horizon, historical data suggests you could expect an average return of around 7-10% annually. However, that's an average over decades, meaning some years will yield higher returns and others may produce losses. Managing expectations based on market norms and historical trends allows you to approach investments with a realistic outlook, reducing the chances of emotional reactions during market downturns.

By aligning your investment strategy with your time horizon and managing expectations, you create a framework that supports your financial goals while accommodating your comfort with risk. Adjusting your portfolio periodically ensures it remains aligned with your current objectives and life circumstances, contributing to a more stable, fulfilling investment experience.

Insurance for Investment Protection

Investment protection extends beyond diversifying assets and managing market risk. It also involves safeguarding against unexpected life events that could derail your financial plans and potentially impact your family's stability. Insurance, therefore, plays a critical role in risk management by providing financial support in the face of illness, accidents, and other unforeseen circumstances. This section explores key types of insurance that can protect both your investments and the well-being of your family: life insurance, property and liability insurance, and health and long-term care insurance. Each form of coverage serves a unique purpose, providing financial peace of mind as you build and protect wealth.

Life Insurance: Types and Benefits; Protecting Family Wealth; When to Consider Life Insurance

Life insurance is a fundamental tool for protecting your family's financial future if something happens to you. Although life insurance doesn't directly increase your wealth, it shields your family from financial hardship in your absence and ensures they can maintain their standard of living. When considering life insurance, it's important to understand the different types available and how each can serve your needs.

Types of Life Insurance

The two main types of life insurance are term life and permanent life insurance. Term life insurance covers you for a specific period, often 10, 20, or 30 years, and is generally more affordable than permanent insurance. It's an ideal choice for individuals who need temporary coverage during key life stages, such as when they have young children or a mortgage to pay. Permanent life insurance, which includes whole and universal life policies, provides lifelong coverage and accumulates cash value over time. Although more expensive than term life, permanent policies can also act as a savings tool, as you can borrow against or withdraw from the cash value under certain conditions. Choosing between term and permanent life insurance depends on your budget, financial goals, and the length of coverage you need.

Protecting Family Wealth

Life insurance is particularly valuable if you have dependents who rely on your income. The death benefit can cover essential expenses, such as mortgage payments, educational costs, and daily living expenses, ensuring that your family isn't left in financial distress. For instance, consider a young parent who passes away unexpectedly. Without life insurance, their spouse may struggle to afford housing and child care, forcing them to make tough financial decisions. Life insurance, however, offers a financial cushion that allows surviving family members to adapt to their new circumstances without facing immediate financial pressure.

When to Consider Life Insurance

While life insurance is often necessary for individuals with dependents, the need for coverage may vary at different life stages. Younger individuals without dependents may not need life insurance right away, while new parents or those with significant debt should prioritize obtaining a policy. Additionally, life insurance is often critical for business owners, as it can be used to support buy-sell agreements or provide financial continuity for the company in the event of the owner's death. As you assess your life insurance needs, consider how your absence would impact your family's financial well-being and determine the coverage that aligns with your situation.

With life insurance in place, you're ensuring that your family's financial goals and stability remain intact, even if unforeseen events occur. By evaluating your needs, you can find a life insurance policy that balances affordability with adequate protection.

Property and Liability Insurance: Coverage for Real Estate; Importance of Liability Protection; Additional Policies

Property and liability insurance are essential components of protecting the assets you've worked hard to acquire, such as real estate and investments. These policies protect not only the physical structures you own but also guard against potential liability claims that could otherwise jeopardize your wealth. Understanding property and liability insurance options can help you maintain financial security while safeguarding your investments.

Coverage for Real Estate

Property insurance, including homeowners and rental property insurance, is crucial for anyone who owns real estate. A standard homeowners insurance policy covers the home structure, personal belongings, and sometimes additional living expenses if the property becomes uninhabitable due to damage. If you own rental properties, landlord insurance provides similar protection but also covers risks unique to renting, such as lost rental income and liability for tenant injuries on the property. These policies ensure that any damage caused by fire, natural disasters, or other covered events doesn't financially devastate you, and they allow for continuity in your investment portfolio. Moreover, if your property is mortgaged, lenders will typically require you to carry adequate property insurance as a condition of the loan.

Importance of Liability Protection

Liability insurance protects you from legal claims made against you for damages or injuries caused by you, your family, or your property. For example, if a visitor slips and falls on your property and sues for medical expenses, liability insurance covers the legal costs and any potential settlements, sparing you from personally covering these expenses. High-net-worth individuals and those with multiple properties should also consider umbrella insurance, which provides an extra layer of liability protection beyond standard homeowners or auto policies. Umbrella policies are particularly valuable because they protect you against costly legal claims that could potentially impact your investments and savings.

Additional Policies to Consider

For property investors, additional types of insurance may be beneficial, including flood insurance, earthquake insurance, or coverage specific to regions prone to natural disasters. While standard homeowners policies may cover some natural events, they often exclude damages caused by floods and earthquakes. If your properties are in areas at risk for these events, it's wise to purchase additional policies to avoid unexpected costs that could damage your financial position. As with any insurance, regularly reviewing and updating policies ensures you maintain sufficient coverage as property values and personal wealth increase.

Property and liability insurance play crucial roles in shielding your assets from damage and litigation. Investing in these policies is an effective way to protect your wealth, keep your investments secure, and maintain peace of mind as you grow your portfolio.

Health and Long-Term Care Insurance: Planning for Healthcare Costs; Protecting Retirement Funds; Understanding Policies

Healthcare costs can be a significant financial burden, especially as you approach retirement. Health insurance and long-term care insurance are essential for mitigating these expenses and protecting the retirement funds you've diligently saved. By planning, you can secure coverage that supports your health needs without compromising your financial stability.

Planning for Healthcare Costs

Healthcare expenses are one of the most significant financial challenges retirees face. Medicare, the federal health insurance program for individuals aged 65 and older, provides basic coverage but doesn't cover everything. Out-of-pocket costs for prescription drugs, routine dental and vision care, and long-term care can still be high, even with Medicare. To prepare for these expenses, some individuals purchase supplemental insurance, also known as Medigap, to cover gaps in Medicare coverage. Another option is to enroll in a Medicare Advantage plan, which often includes additional benefits. Planning for healthcare expenses early allows you to budget for premiums and co-pays, ensuring that medical costs don't erode your retirement savings.

Protecting Retirement Funds with Long-Term Care Insurance

Long-term care insurance is designed to cover the costs of assistance with daily activities, such as bathing, dressing, and eating, which many people require as they age. These services are often provided in nursing homes, assisted living facilities, or in-home care settings, and they're typically not covered by Medicare. Without long-term care insurance, the high cost of these services can rapidly deplete your retirement funds. For instance, a year in a nursing home can cost tens of thousands of dollars, potentially undoing years of careful financial planning. By securing long-term care insurance, you protect your retirement savings, ensuring you can access the care you need without compromising your financial security or burdening family members.

Understanding Health and Long-Term Care Policies

Choosing the right health and long-term care insurance policies requires evaluating coverage options, premiums, and benefits. When reviewing health insurance plans, consider factors such as network providers, prescription drug coverage, and out-of-pocket maximums. With long-term care insurance, focus on the daily or monthly benefit amount, benefit duration, and elimination period (the time you must wait before benefits kick in). Some individuals purchase hybrid life and long-term care policies, which combine life insurance with long-term care benefits. These policies offer a death benefit if long-term care is never needed, providing a versatile solution for retirement planning.

Health and long-term care insurance play essential roles in financial planning for retirement. By securing the right coverage, you can protect your retirement funds from unexpected healthcare costs and ensure you receive quality care if you need assistance with daily activities.

Diversification for Risk Reduction

Diversification is one of the most effective strategies to reduce risk and protect your portfolio from major losses. By spreading your investments across different asset classes and categories, you're better equipped to handle market fluctuations and potential downturns in any particular sector. This section explores the essential elements of diversification, including the benefits of spreading risk, incorporating alternative investments, and regularly rebalancing your portfolio to maintain stability and achieve long-term financial health.

Investment Diversification: Benefits of Diversifying; Spreading Risk; Balancing Asset Types

Diversifying your investments means distributing your money across various asset types, industries, and geographical regions to minimize the impact of a poor-performing investment on your overall portfolio. Imagine you have all your funds in one stock, and that company experiences a severe downturn — the consequences for your portfolio could be catastrophic. However, if you have spread your investments among several assets, the loss from one stock is likely to be offset by the gains in others, softening the impact and reducing overall risk.

Benefits of Diversifying

The primary benefit of diversification is risk reduction. By holding a mix of stocks, bonds, and other assets, you're less vulnerable to a single adverse event. Diversification also brings smoother, more consistent returns over time. For instance, while equities might be highly volatile, bonds tend to provide stability. A diversified portfolio often shows fewer fluctuations, as the performance of different asset classes tends to balance out over time. Another key advantage is that diversification provides a level of protection during economic downturns. In times of market stress, various assets behave differently — while stock prices may drop, bonds often retain their value or even increase, providing a cushion.

Spreading Risk Across Different Investments

True diversification involves spreading your investments across different categories, not just different assets within a category. For example, it's not enough to invest in multiple stocks if they're all within the same industry; you'll still be exposed to risks specific to that sector. Instead, consider stocks across various industries, such as technology, healthcare, and consumer goods, to create a more balanced approach. Additionally, international diversification — investing in both domestic and foreign markets — can further reduce risk, as economic conditions in one country may differ significantly from another.

Balancing Asset Types for Stability

When building a diversified portfolio, balancing asset types is essential. Generally, this means including a combination of stocks, bonds, and cash equivalents. Stocks offer growth potential but carry higher risks, while bonds provide stability and regular income, albeit with lower returns. Cash equivalents, such as money market funds, offer liquidity and safety but yield little to no growth. The allocation of these assets should reflect your risk tolerance and investment goals. A younger investor might have a portfolio heavily weighted toward stocks for growth, while a retiree may prefer bonds to preserve capital and generate income.

By diversifying your investments, you spread the risk across a range of assets and create a buffer against losses in any one area, providing a strong foundation for long-term wealth building.

Alternative Investments: Exploring Alternatives (Commodities, REITs); Pros and Cons; How They Add Protection

While traditional assets like stocks and bonds form the backbone of many portfolios, alternative investments can enhance diversification and potentially protect against market volatility. Alternatives — which include commodities, real estate investment trusts (REITs), and private equity — offer unique benefits and risks, making them valuable additions to a diversified portfolio.

Exploring Alternative Investments

Alternative investments refer to non-traditional assets that don't fall into the typical categories of stocks, bonds, or cash. Commodities, such as gold, silver, and oil, often move independently of stock markets, providing a hedge against inflation and currency fluctuations. Real Estate Investment Trusts (REITs) allow investors to gain exposure to real estate markets without owning physical property, offering a steady income stream and potential for capital appreciation. Private equity and hedge funds also fall under the alternative investment umbrella, though they typically require larger capital commitments and may be less accessible to average investors.

Pros and Cons of Alternatives

One advantage of alternative investments is their low correlation with the stock market. When stocks are down, alternatives like gold or REITs may still hold or increase in value, offering protection and stability. Additionally, certain alternatives, such as REITs and commodities, provide inflation protection. However, alternatives can also carry higher fees and require a more complex understanding. They're often less liquid than traditional investments, meaning it may be harder to sell them quickly. Furthermore, the returns on alternatives can be highly variable. While some, like gold, may act as a haven, others, such as private equity, involve significant risks and long lock-in periods, making them more suitable for investors with a higher tolerance for risk.

Adding Protection with Alternative Investments

Incorporating alternative investments adds a layer of protection to your portfolio by balancing out the performance of traditional assets. For example, when inflation rises, commodity prices, particularly for gold and oil, tend to increase as well. This counters the negative effects that inflation may have on stocks and bonds. Meanwhile, REITs provide both income and potential capital appreciation, offering returns similar to stocks with the stability often associated with real estate. By strategically adding alternative investments, you further diversify your portfolio, reducing overall risk and protecting against downturns in the stock market.

Alternatives enhance the resilience of your portfolio, offering a safeguard during economic turbulence. With careful selection, alternative investments can be a powerful component of a well-diversified portfolio.

Rebalancing for Stability: When to Rebalance; Maintaining Desired Risk Level; Ensuring Portfolio Health

Diversification is most effective when paired with regular portfolio rebalancing. Over time, the value of different assets fluctuates, potentially altering the balance of your portfolio and exposing you to unintended risk levels. Rebalancing is the process of realigning your portfolio back to its original asset allocation, ensuring that you maintain the risk profile aligned with your goals.

When to Rebalance Your Portfolio

Rebalancing should occur at regular intervals, whether quarterly, biannually, or annually, depending on your preference and market conditions. Additionally, significant market movements — such as a major stock market rally or downturn — may prompt the need for rebalancing, as these fluctuations can cause certain assets to become overrepresented in your portfolio. For example, if stocks perform exceptionally well, they may constitute a larger portion of your portfolio than intended, increasing your exposure to market volatility. Rebalancing restores your portfolio to its target allocation, ensuring it reflects your initial risk tolerance.

Maintaining the Desired Risk Level

The purpose of rebalancing is to keep your portfolio aligned with your risk tolerance and investment goals. Without rebalancing, you may unknowingly take on more risk than intended. Imagine a portfolio with an initial allocation of 60% stocks and 40% bonds. If stocks experience significant gains, they might grow to 70% of the portfolio's value. While this increase is positive in terms of returns, it also means that your portfolio is now more heavily exposed to stock market risk than originally planned. By rebalancing, you can sell a portion of the stocks and reinvest the proceeds into bonds, restoring the desired balance and maintaining a level of risk that feels comfortable and manageable.

Ensuring Portfolio Health and Long-Term Stability
Rebalancing not only maintains your desired risk level but also promotes long-term portfolio health. This process allows you to lock in gains from overperforming assets while reinvesting in underperforming ones at a lower cost, a practice known as "selling high and buying low." Furthermore, by periodically reassessing your asset allocation and rebalancing, you can make necessary adjustments as your life circumstances or financial goals evolve. For instance, as you near retirement, you may want to shift more funds into bonds and other conservative investments, reducing your exposure to stock market volatility and preserving your wealth.

In essence, rebalancing is about ensuring that your portfolio remains in good shape over time, sustaining its alignment with your goals and risk tolerance. It's a disciplined approach that keeps your investments on track and preserves the integrity of your diversified strategy.

Chapter 8: Financial Independence

Achieving financial independence is a profound and life-changing goal that requires thoughtful planning, disciplined habits, and a clear understanding of what it truly means to be financially free. Financial independence can look different for everyone — for some, it means retiring early and pursuing passions; for others, it's about having enough wealth to provide security and flexibility in life choices. In this chapter, we'll explore how to set financial freedom goals, create a lifestyle that supports sustainable wealth, and visualize a roadmap to help you reach each milestone.

Defining Financial Independence: What It Means; Realistic Milestones; Setting Measurable Goals

Financial independence, at its core, is the ability to cover your living expenses without relying on earned income. This means you have built enough wealth, often through investments, that generate enough income to support your needs and desires. The journey to financial independence is highly personal, as it's not just about accumulating wealth but also about aligning your finances with your ideal lifestyle and values.

What Financial Independence Really Means

Financial independence doesn't necessarily mean quitting your job; it's about having the freedom to choose whether you want to work or pursue other passions. For some, it's the capacity to travel, spend time with loved ones, or engage in meaningful work without the stress of financial constraints. The meaning of financial independence may shift over time as personal circumstances change. What's consistent, however, is that reaching financial independence provides control and flexibility — you're not bound by the need to work solely for income but can make life choices that bring you fulfillment and joy.

Setting Realistic Milestones

Financial independence is rarely an all-or-nothing goal; it's achieved through a series of realistic milestones. For example, the first milestone may be creating an emergency fund that covers three to six months of expenses, which builds a solid safety net. The next milestone might be paying off high-interest debts, as debt can be a major obstacle to financial freedom. From there, goals could include achieving a specific net worth, building passive income streams that cover a portion of your expenses, or eventually accumulating enough wealth to cover all your essential and discretionary spending. By setting incremental milestones, you stay motivated and maintain a clear path toward complete financial independence.

Creating Measurable Goals

To make financial independence achievable, define your goals in measurable terms. Instead of a vague goal like "I want to be financially independent," specify an amount of passive income you aim to generate each month or the net worth you believe will comfortably support your lifestyle. This makes it easier to track progress and adjust as needed. The SMART goal framework — setting goals that are Specific, Measurable, Achievable, Relevant, and Time-bound — is invaluable here. For instance, you might set a goal to "generate $2,000 a month in passive income by investing in dividend stocks over the next five years." This is measurable, specific, and gives you a clear target.

When you define financial independence in personal terms, with realistic milestones and measurable goals, the journey becomes clearer, making each step toward financial freedom purposeful and fulfilling.

Building a Sustainable Lifestyle: Balancing Spending and Saving; Reducing Debt; Financial Habits for Freedom

While building wealth is essential to achieving financial independence, sustaining that wealth requires a lifestyle that balances saving, spending, and smart financial decisions. Building a sustainable lifestyle means creating habits that support long-term freedom and protecting the assets that enable it.

Balancing Spending and Saving

To reach financial independence, it's important to strike a balance between enjoying life now and preparing for the future. This doesn't mean a life of frugality; rather, it's about prioritizing spending on things that genuinely add value and bring happiness, while avoiding unnecessary expenses. Creating a budget based on your values and long-term goals can help guide your spending. A common guideline is the 50/30/20 rule: allocate 50% of your income to needs, 30% to wants, and 20% to savings or debt repayment. This rule can be adjusted based on individual circumstances, but the principle remains — live within your means, save consistently, and invest wisely.

Reducing Debt

Debt can be a significant barrier to financial independence, particularly high-interest debt, which can erode wealth. A key step toward financial freedom is identifying and tackling debt strategically. Start by focusing on high-interest debts, such as credit card balances, as they tend to accumulate quickly and have a substantial impact on your finances. The "debt avalanche" method, where you pay off debts with the highest interest rates first, can be effective in minimizing interest costs. Alternatively, the "debt snowball" method, where you pay off smaller debts first, can provide psychological wins and momentum. By eliminating or reducing debt, you free up resources to invest and build wealth rather than losing income to interest payments.

Developing Financial Habits for Freedom

Financial independence is not only a matter of wealth but also of financial habits that sustain it. Developing a habit of budgeting, tracking expenses, and regularly reviewing your financial plan can keep you on the path to financial independence. Additionally, automating savings and investments can ensure consistent progress. It's helpful to set aside a portion of each paycheck for investments before allocating money to other expenses. This habit, often called "paying yourself first," prioritizes your financial future and helps grow your wealth over time.

By building a lifestyle that balances present enjoyment with future security, and by reducing debt and adopting financial habits that support your goals, you create a strong foundation for lasting financial freedom.

Visualizing Your Path: Creating a Roadmap; Identifying Key Steps; Setting Timelines

Visualizing your journey to financial independence can provide clarity and motivation, making the process feel more achievable. Creating a roadmap helps break down the larger goal into manageable steps, each with a specific timeline that keeps you on track and focused.

Creating a Roadmap to Financial Independence

A roadmap to financial independence is a strategic plan that outlines the steps and milestones needed to achieve your goal. Start by identifying where you are now, including your current financial standing, assets, debts, and income. Then, envision where you want to be at each stage of your journey. For example, your roadmap might include stages like building an emergency fund, reaching a certain level of passive income, or achieving a target investment portfolio size. This roadmap should align with the realistic milestones and measurable goals you set previously. By charting your progress over time, you can see how each step brings you closer to your ultimate goal.

Identifying Key Steps in Your Journey

Within your roadmap, identify the key steps that will have the most impact on your progress. For instance, if you're early in your journey, focusing on debt reduction and creating a budget might be your priorities. As you gain financial stability, you might shift your focus to building an investment portfolio or purchasing income-generating assets. Recognize that each key step is a building block toward financial independence, and allow time to celebrate progress along the way. Financial independence is a marathon, not a sprint; acknowledging the completion of each stage helps sustain motivation and commitment.

Setting Timelines for Each Milestone

Timelines give structure to your roadmap and provide a sense of urgency. Set realistic deadlines for each financial milestone based on your income, savings rate, and investment goals. For instance, if your first goal is to save an emergency fund equivalent to three months of expenses, calculate how much you need to save monthly to reach that goal within a set period, such as one year. As you progress, you may set timelines for other milestones, such as investing a certain amount each year or achieving a specific net worth by a target date. However, it's essential to remain flexible; life changes may require adjustments to your timeline. Financial independence is a journey that requires patience, and it's okay to adjust your course as circumstances evolve.

Visualizing your path to financial independence and setting actionable timelines makes the goal feel concrete and achievable, helping you stay committed even when faced with challenges.

Staying on Track

Once you have set your financial independence goals and established a path forward, the next crucial step is staying on course. Financial independence is not a one-time decision but a long-term journey that requires dedication, adaptability, and ongoing learning. This section focuses on ways to track your progress, adjust for life changes, and continuously grow your knowledge to maintain motivation and momentum.

Tracking Progress: Using Tools to Monitor; Making Adjustments; Staying Motivated

Achieving financial independence involves monitoring your progress regularly to ensure you're on track to reach your goals. By staying aware of where you are concerning your milestones, you can make informed decisions and maintain the motivation to continue your journey.

Using Tools to Monitor Progress

One of the most effective ways to stay on track is by using financial tools to monitor your progress. Tools like budgeting apps, net worth trackers, and investment portfolio managers can provide clear insights into your financial health and trajectory. Budgeting apps help you keep track of income, expenses, and savings, giving you a real-time view of how well you're aligning with your financial plan. Net worth trackers allow you to see how your assets are growing over time, while investment portfolio managers help ensure that your investments align with your goals and risk tolerance. Regularly using these tools can give you a strong sense of control over your finances and allow you to make any necessary adjustments before small issues become big setbacks.

Making Adjustments as Needed

Staying on track requires flexibility. Even with a solid plan, market conditions, income fluctuations, or changes in personal circumstances can affect your progress. When monitoring your finances, you may identify areas that require adjustment, whether that's reducing expenses, reallocating investments, or increasing savings in response to a higher-than-expected expense. For instance, if a market downturn affects your portfolio, you might consider shifting funds into safer, more stable investments or temporarily increasing contributions to make up for any losses. Making adjustments as you go ensures that your plan remains relevant and aligned with both your current situation and your long-term goals.

Staying Motivated

Motivation is essential to staying the course, especially during challenging times. Achieving financial independence is a marathon, not a sprint, and maintaining motivation over years or even decades can be difficult. To keep your momentum, break larger goals into smaller milestones that can be celebrated along the way. Each milestone—such as reaching an emergency fund goal, paying off a debt, or hitting a new net worth level—serves as a reminder of the progress you're making. Additionally, try to surround yourself with a supportive network of like-minded individuals who value financial independence, as they can provide encouragement and insight when you need it most. Tracking your progress, celebrating milestones, and finding motivation in your achievements all contribute to a rewarding and fulfilling journey.

Adjusting for Life Changes: Adapting Plans for Life Events; Flexibility in Financial Plans; Balancing Stability and Change

Life is unpredictable, and financial independence plans must be flexible enough to adapt to significant life events. Whether you experience changes in career, family dynamics, health, or personal goals, a resilient financial plan can accommodate these shifts while keeping you on course for financial freedom.

Adapting Plans for Major Life Events

Major life changes, such as marriage, the birth of a child, career changes, or unexpected health issues, can affect your finances significantly. In these instances, it's essential to revisit your financial independence goals and adjust them to reflect your new priorities. For instance, if you have children, you may want to save for their education, which could require reallocating resources or adjusting your investment strategy.

Similarly, a career change may result in an income shift, prompting you to recalibrate your budget and investment contributions. Being proactive in assessing the impact of these life events and modifying your plan accordingly can ensure that your path to financial independence remains realistic and achievable.

Maintaining Flexibility in Financial Plans

Flexibility is crucial in a financial independence plan. Life circumstances change, and financial markets can be volatile; having a rigid plan might leave you vulnerable to these shifts. By building flexibility into your plan, you can better navigate unexpected events without derailing your progress. For example, maintaining a diverse portfolio with a mix of liquid and long-term assets can provide options in times of need. Additionally, revisiting your budget periodically allows you to make incremental adjustments rather than overhauling your entire plan. This flexibility provides a balance between staying committed to your goals and having the adaptability to manage unforeseen circumstances.

Balancing Stability with Change

While flexibility is essential, so is stability. The key to a successful financial independence plan is to strike a balance between making necessary adjustments and staying committed to your overall goals. Certain aspects of your plan, such as retirement savings or emergency funds, should remain stable, even if other parts of your budget fluctuate. This stability ensures that core components of your financial independence strategy are always in place, providing a safety net for your future. By focusing on maintaining a steady foundation while making adjustments as needed, you create a sustainable path that can weather life's inevitable changes.

Continuous Learning: Keeping Up with Financial Trends; Importance of Personal Growth; Staying Informed

Financial independence is a dynamic journey, and staying informed about changes in the financial landscape can make a significant difference in achieving your goals. From understanding new investment options to staying aware of tax law changes, continuous learning is essential to making informed decisions and maintaining a robust financial plan.

Keeping Up with Financial Trends

The financial world is constantly evolving, and staying updated on trends can help you take advantage of new opportunities or avoid potential pitfalls. For example, understanding recent trends in technology, renewable energy, or emerging markets can provide insights into potential investment opportunities. Following reputable financial news sources, subscribing to industry newsletters, or attending financial seminars can provide a broader perspective on what's happening in the market and how it may impact your financial independence plan. Keeping up with these trends allows you to make informed decisions that align with current economic conditions and long-term prospects.

The Importance of Personal Growth

Achieving financial independence often requires more than just sound financial management; it involves personal growth and development. This growth may include developing better financial habits, building resilience during tough economic times, and learning from any mistakes made along the way. Personal growth also means building confidence in your financial decisions and cultivating a mindset that embraces discipline and patience. Financial independence is as much about character as it is about strategy. A growth mindset, focused on continuous improvement, allows you to evolve alongside your financial journey, adapting to new knowledge and applying it to your plan.

Staying Informed for Better Decision-Making

Knowledge is power when it comes to financial independence. Staying informed about tax changes, shifts in the economy, or new investment tools can help you make better choices that benefit your financial goals. For instance, being aware of tax-advantaged retirement account changes can allow you to adjust your contributions and maximize tax benefits. Similarly, understanding fluctuations in interest rates or inflation levels can guide your decisions on when to buy property or invest in bonds. Making a habit of reviewing your financial plan and keeping it up-to-date with current information helps you stay agile and prepared for both opportunities and challenges.

Continuous learning, personal growth, and staying informed allow you to make well-rounded financial decisions that support your independence journey. By expanding your knowledge, you equip yourself with the tools and confidence needed to navigate the complexities of the financial world.

Leaving a Legacy

As you approach financial independence, it's not just about securing your future; it's also about ensuring that your financial success has a lasting impact beyond your lifetime. Leaving a legacy involves protecting your wealth, educating your heirs, and aligning your financial choices with your values. This section explores the fundamentals of estate planning, the importance of teaching financial literacy to your family, and how to create a meaningful, lasting legacy that extends far beyond your own financial goals.

Estate Planning Basics: Importance of Wills and Trusts; Protecting Wealth for Heirs; Making Charitable Decisions

Estate planning is one of the most important steps in ensuring that the wealth you've worked hard to build is transferred according to your wishes. A well-structured estate plan can provide peace of mind for both you and your loved ones, ensuring that your assets are distributed effectively and in a way that honors your goals.

Importance of Wills and Trusts

At the heart of any estate plan is a will, a legal document that outlines your wishes regarding the distribution of your assets after your death. Without a will, your estate could be subject to state laws, which may not align with your desires. A will ensures that your property, investments, and other assets go to the people or organizations you care about most. However, there are limitations to wills. For example, they often go through probate, a legal process that can take time and incur costs.

This is where trusts come in. A trust is a legal arrangement where a trustee holds and manages your assets on behalf of your beneficiaries. Trusts can help avoid probate, reduce estate taxes, and provide greater control over how and when your heirs receive their inheritance. Trusts come in various forms, such as revocable or irrevocable, and each offers different levels of control and flexibility. A revocable trust can be altered or revoked during your lifetime, while an irrevocable trust cannot, providing a greater degree of asset protection.

In addition to these basic tools, you might also consider setting up powers of attorney for health and finances, as well as advance healthcare directives. These documents ensure that your wishes are honored should you become incapacitated and unable to make decisions for yourself.

Protecting Wealth for Heirs

Beyond the distribution of assets, estate planning also involves taking steps to protect the wealth you've accumulated for your heirs. One of the key challenges of passing on wealth is minimizing the tax burden on your estate and your beneficiaries. Estate taxes can be significant, depending on the value of your estate, and can reduce the amount your heirs receive. One way to reduce these taxes is by gifting assets to your heirs during your lifetime, thus reducing the overall value of your estate. You can also explore tax-deferred accounts, like certain life insurance policies, to protect wealth from tax erosion.

Moreover, estate planning allows you to ensure that your heirs are financially prepared to manage their inheritance. This can include setting up a trust that offers financial support to younger beneficiaries or providing them with the tools and knowledge they need to make smart decisions about managing wealth.

Making Charitable Decisions

Another important aspect of estate planning is deciding whether to include charitable contributions as part of your legacy. Many people wish to give back to causes that are meaningful to them, and charitable giving can be a powerful way to make a lasting impact on the world. Charitable giving can be incorporated into your estate plan through charitable trusts, donor-advised funds, or direct bequests to charities. Not only does this allow you to leave a positive impact, but it can also provide tax benefits during your lifetime, reducing the size of your taxable estate.

Teaching Financial Literacy: Educating Family Members; Passing on Wealth-Building Knowledge; Creating Financial Stability for Others

Financial literacy is one of the greatest gifts you can pass on to your children, grandchildren, or any other heirs. Teaching the next generation about managing money, investing, and making sound financial decisions can help them build wealth and secure their financial independence. This section highlights the importance of educating your family about money and providing them with the tools they need to make responsible financial decisions.

Educating Family Members

Start by having open conversations about money. Many people shy away from discussing finances with their family members, but doing so can break down barriers and help everyone understand the financial landscape. Share your financial journey with them—how you made decisions, what you learned from your mistakes, and the strategies that have worked for you. Open discussions create an atmosphere of trust, where financial education is normalized and valued.

Additionally, consider providing formal financial education to your family members. You can teach them basic principles of budgeting, saving, investing, and debt management. These lessons can be delivered through family meetings, workshops, or by encouraging them to read books and take courses on personal finance. Financial literacy isn't just about numbers; it's about developing the mindset that money is a tool to achieve long-term goals and financial independence.

Passing on Wealth-Building Knowledge

To ensure that your heirs don't just inherit money, but also the wisdom to build wealth, you can provide them with guidance on long-term financial planning. Teach them how to approach money not just for immediate needs, but with an eye toward sustainable growth. This involves instilling a mindset that values investments, encourages disciplined saving, and emphasizes the importance of diversifying assets.

Passing on wealth-building knowledge might also mean helping your children or grandchildren get started with their investments. For example, you can open a custodial account for younger heirs, where you guide them on the principles of investing. Let them make some of the decisions under your supervision to gain experience and confidence. This can prepare them to take on more responsibility in managing their finances as they grow older.

Creating Financial Stability for Others

Teaching financial literacy isn't just about giving financial advice; it's about helping others become financially self-sufficient. Providing them with the tools they need to create and maintain financial stability ensures that they can support themselves and build their wealth, regardless of the resources they pass down. For some, this might mean helping them develop a career path or providing initial capital for entrepreneurial endeavors. For others, it might involve offering ongoing guidance as they navigate complex financial decisions. Ultimately, the goal is to ensure that your heirs don't rely solely on an inheritance but have the knowledge and confidence to create their financial future.

Building a Lasting Impact: Importance of Financial Values; Aligning Investments with Ethics; Leaving a Meaningful Legacy

Leaving a legacy isn't just about wealth—it's about the values and principles you pass down through your actions. The investments you choose, the charitable causes you support, and the way you manage your finances all send a message about what you stand for. This section discusses the importance of aligning your investments with your values and creating a lasting, meaningful impact.

The Importance of Financial Values

As you approach financial independence, consider what values matter most to you and how they can shape your financial decisions. Do you care about environmental sustainability? Social justice? Corporate responsibility? Financial independence offers the opportunity to align your wealth with your values. For example, you can invest in companies or funds that reflect your commitment to sustainability, or support industries that foster positive social change. Aligning your financial choices with your values doesn't just make you feel good—it also creates a legacy that reflects your principles and inspires others to consider the broader impact of their financial decisions.

Aligning Investments with Ethics

Ethical investing, also known as socially responsible investing (SRI) or impact investing, is becoming an increasingly popular way to ensure that your wealth is invested in companies or projects that align with your personal beliefs. For example, if you care about environmental sustainability, you may choose to invest in green energy or companies that focus on reducing their carbon footprint. If social equity is important to you, you might invest in funds that support gender equality, fair wages, or affordable housing.

Impact investing allows you to create wealth while making a positive difference in the world. It ensures that your financial legacy isn't just about monetary gain but also about contributing to the betterment of society.

Leaving a Meaningful Legacy

Finally, leaving a meaningful legacy means ensuring that the impact of your wealth endures beyond your lifetime. This can be done through charitable giving, supporting causes that matter to you, or creating funds that continue your values. By thinking carefully about how your wealth is distributed, whether to family members or charitable organizations, you create a legacy that reflects your life's work and the things you care most about. Your financial legacy can serve as a blueprint for others to follow, providing them with the tools to continue the work you started and inspire future generations to create lasting, positive change.

Final Chapter: A Word of Advice and Gratitude

As we come to the end of this journey toward financial independence, I want to take a moment to thank you for your attention and commitment to learning. Achieving financial independence is not an easy task, and it requires consistent effort, discipline, and patience. But the knowledge you've gained throughout this book, combined with the actions you take, will empower you to take control of your financial future and pave the way for lasting success.

A Word of Advice

One of the most important pieces of advice I can offer is to start today. Regardless of where you are in your financial journey, the earlier you begin, the more time you have to grow your wealth. It's easy to get caught up in the idea that there's a "perfect time" to start investing, but the truth is that the best time is always now. Even if you can only save or invest a small amount, consistency is key. Remember, the power of compounding works in your favor over time.

Stay disciplined in your approach. Financial independence is not about taking shortcuts or chasing the latest trends in the market. It's about making informed decisions, diversifying your investments, and sticking to your strategy even when the market seems unpredictable. Focus on the long term, and be prepared to adjust your approach when necessary. Your financial plan should be flexible enough to evolve with changes in your life, but strong enough to keep you on track toward your ultimate goals.

Educate yourself continually. Financial knowledge is the foundation of financial freedom, and the more you learn, the better equipped you'll be to make decisions that benefit your future. Take the time to read books, listen to podcasts, or even work with a financial advisor to enhance your understanding. The landscape of investing and personal finance is always changing, and staying informed will give you the edge you need to make smart decisions.

Lastly, don't forget to enjoy the process. Achieving financial independence isn't just about accumulating wealth; it's about living a life that aligns with your values and goals. Make sure that the journey towards your financial freedom is fulfilling, and take time to appreciate your progress. Whether it's spending more time with family, traveling, or pursuing a passion, financial independence gives you the freedom to live life on your terms. Make the most of it.

Gratitude for Your Attention

I want to sincerely thank you for taking the time to read this book and invest in your financial future. Your commitment to learning and improving your financial knowledge is commendable, and it is a critical step toward achieving the freedom you desire. Financial independence is not just about securing your own future; it's about having the freedom to make choices that bring you happiness, security, and peace of mind. The journey may not always be smooth, but with determination, smart planning, and the right mindset, you can reach your destination.

Remember, the road to financial independence is a marathon, not a sprint. Stay patient, stay focused, and, most importantly, stay true to your goals. Thank you again for your attention and for allowing me to be a part of your journey. I wish you success in all your financial endeavors and the peace of mind that comes with knowing you are in control of your financial future.

www.ingramcontent.com/pod-product-compliance
Lightning Source LLC
Chambersburg PA
CBHW052352220526
45465CB00003BA/1078

Félix Vidalin

L'Agriculture et la vie rurale en Italie

Essai

 Le code de la propriété intellectuelle du 1er juillet 1992 interdit en effet expressément la photocopie à usage collectif sans autorisation des ayants droit. Or, cette pratique s'est généralisée dans les établissements d'enseignement supérieur, provoquant une baisse brutale des achats de livres et de revues, au point que la possibilité même pour les auteurs de créer des œuvres nouvelles et de les faire éditer correctement est aujourd'hui menacée. En application de la loi du 11 mars 1957, il est interdit de reproduire intégralement ou partiellement le présent ouvrage, sur quelque support que ce soit, sans autorisation de l'Éditeur ou du Centre Français d'Exploitation du Droit de Copie , 20, rue Grands Augustins, 75006 Paris.

ISBN : 978-1978092877

10 9 8 7 6 5 4 3 2 1